I0449731

Murder in America

Correlates of
Murder and Race as a Factor

by

Jack Frymier and Arliss Roaden

authorHOUSE™

1663 Liberty Drive, Suite 200
Bloomington, Indiana 47403
(800) 839-8640
www.AuthorHouse.com

© 2005 Jack Frymier and Arliss Roaden. All Rights Reserved.

No part of this book may be reproduced, stored in a retrieval system, or transmitted by any means without the written permission of the author.

First published by AuthorHouse 02/21/05

ISBN: 1-4208-1599-7 (e)
ISBN: 1-4208-1598-9 (sc)

Printed in the United States of America
Bloomington, Indiana

This book is printed on acid-free paper.

Jack Frymier   Arliss Roaden
Professor Emeritus   President Emeritus
The Ohio State University   Tennessee Technological University

For additional information about this project contact

Jack Frymier
5367 Flatrock Court
Morrison, CO 80465

303-697-0558

Table of Contents

Preface

This study of murder in America developed over time from a casual interest to intense commitment. We wanted to understand some of the dynamics at work in our society. During the past fifteen years, our research focus has evolved from studying young people at risk to values and ethical conduct to problems of urban schools to funding public education to policymaking at the state level to comparing states on these and other factors. Last year we published *Cultures of the States: A Handbook on the Effectiveness of State Government* (Lanham, Maryland and Oxford: The Scarecrow Press, Inc., 2003. 411 pp.) We think of ourselves as students of human behavior—what people do, and why they do what they do—and in the last five years we have accumulated a huge database related specifically to diverse human activities within each of the fifty states on working and earning, living and dying, abiding by or flouting the law, learning, voting, smoking, procreating, and a host of other things that make those of us who call ourselves Americans who we really are.

This monograph is actually the sixth project that we have attempted along these lines. The first was titled *Violence in America,* and in that project we began with a double-barreled assumption: murder is violent, and highway deaths are violent. The way to study violence in America, we thought, would be to use these two variables as criterion measures to identify violent states, then compare more violent states with less violent states on hundreds of other variables to see if and how those two groups of states might differ.

We did that study, produced that report (i.e., *Violence in America*), shared the report with a few friends, and immediately began to work on other analyses that had to do with how states differed on the basis of such things as taxation rates, high school graduation rates, and voter participation in elections. Then we began to wonder: Were the analyses regarding murder and highway fatalities appropriate? Were the findings valid? Were the conclusions that we drew defensible?

Our wonder turned to worry. Maybe the assumptions we made and the processes we employed were appropriate empirically but not logically. There seemed to be no doubt that both murder and highway fatalities could be described with accuracy as instances of "violence," but most murders were the result of intentional behaviors, and almost all highway fatalities were the result of behaviors that were accidental and unintentional. That caused us, in the parlance of another field, "to go back to the drawing board," so back we went.

Originally, we had been uncomfortable with terminology used by the Federal Bureau of Investigation and the Department of Justice to describe "violent crime." Specifically, there are eight categories of crime, as defined by the Federal Bureau of Investigation: murder, assault, rape, robbery, burglary, larceny, motor vehicle theft, and arson. The first four—murder, assault, rape, and robbery—are categorized as "violent crime," and the other four are labeled "property crime." Reports from the federal government generally "add" statistics on murder, assault, rape, and robbery to produce a summation statistic on "violent crime" in a particular community or state. But there were always many more instances of robbery than murder, no matter how we looked at the numbers, and murder was always "worse" than robbery, in our minds, so we were reluctant to "add up" such instances and call the summation "violent crime." There was logic to the summation process, but even though robbery might involve taking property from a person by use of intimidation or force, the idea that "one robbery" was in any way equivalent to "one murder," or that the two could be added together to produce "two violent crimes" did not make sense to us. It was that mental discomfort that led us to put murders and highway fatalities together under the general rubric of "violence" in the first place.

But then we realized that, even though murders and highway fatalities might both be "violent" and both involve the loss of life, because one was deliberate and criminal and the other accidental and not criminal, we needed to rethink the basic assumptions of our analyses.

So we decided to start over. We thought, however, that we should redo the study of highway fatalities first, so we separated the 50 states on the basis of highway fatalities according to two criteria: traffic fatalities per 100,000 population in 1999, and percent change in traffic fatalities from 1975 to 1999. Any state that ranked in the top half of both of these tables (see Table G.343 and Table G.345 in the *Cultures* book, described above) was assumed to be a "high traffic fatality" state (N = 18), and the remaining states were assumed to be "low traffic fatality" states (N = 32). We then compared high traffic fatality states with low traffic fatality states on more than 400 variables, and produced our second report: *Violent Deaths on the Highways*.

After that, we established criteria regarding violence in various ways. First, we rank-ordered all 50 states on the four "violence" variables used by the Federal Bureau of Investigation: murder, rape, assault, and robbery. Any state listed in the top half of all four rankings was assumed to be "high" on violent crimes. Fifteen states were identified by this process, and following analyses comparing those 15 states with the other 35 states, 113 variables were found to discriminate between the "high violent crime states" and "low violent crime states."

Second, we selected two of those same four variables—murder and assault—and proceeded to identify every state in the top half of both of those rankings, then assumed that those states were "more violent" and the remaining states "less violent." Nineteen high violence states were identified by this process, and 146 variables discriminated between the 19 high violent states and the 31 low violent states at a statistically significant level.

Third, we rank-ordered all 50 states on just one variable—murder—then identified the top 16 states as high murder rate states and the remaining 34 as low murder rate states. In those analyses, 148 variables discriminated between the high and low murder rate states.

Finally, we used the same rank-ordering process described in step three above, but drew the line to separate high murder rate and low murder rate groups in the middle of that ranking, producing one group of high murder rate states and one group of low murder rate states, with 25 states in each group. Approximately 135 variables discriminated statistically in the analyses that we then accomplished. The present monograph, *Murder in America*, reports the results of this fourth set of analyses. The results of the first, second, and third set of analyses described above have not been reported, but we have the printouts available for anyone who wishes to see them.

If you ask "Why did you decide to report the analyses accomplished in the fourth study (i.e., actually the sixth analysis of these same data, counting the first two analyses described above) rather than all of the other analyses?" our answer is simple, though it may not be satisfactory to you: it seemed most reasonable and defensible to us.

We share this whole process because we think it is important for you to know how we got to where we are right now; about to share details of a study based on murder rates in America over a 39-year time period with you. All of these analyses were interesting in their own right, but three things emerged in the process that led us to decide to report the data that are included here. First, our understanding of "violence" broadened and deepened as we became aware of certain basic differences in "violence" implicit in the definitions and data about both murder and highway deaths, as described above. Second, the statistical relationships of highway fatalities with taxes collected by states are more than obvious in *Violent Death on the Highways*; they are prominent. Third, the statistical relationships of murder rates with taxes collected by states is almost nil. Those data are reported here, and they may describe what policymakers in state government already know and deal with, or they may be something with which they are only vaguely familiar. We hope this study will be helpful along that line.

Through these processes we settled on the idea of studying the crime of murder in our society. After we had analyzed the data and begun to think about how we could put it all together in a meaningful way, our first intention was "to walk the reader through" the project in a logical manner: problem to procedures to data to findings to conclusions. We put it together that way, but the story seemed so jumbled and complex as to be almost nonsensical. Part of that was because we looked at so many "pieces" of society in relation to murder that it was overwhelming. Part of it was probably our inability to sort out the important from the unimportant, or maybe it was our bumbling nature with words. Whatever it was, we decided to back up and try to put it together again in a way that made sense to us, and that we hoped would make sense to you.

We are very sensitive to the fact that what follows is complex. We describe the problem of murder in America first, as we see it, then how we studied the problem. After that we discuss what we found in the study, but we placed all of the specific findings in appendices at the back of the book, along with the tables that report the results of analyses that were accomplished. We think the numbers are very important, but we realize that numbers "get in the way" for many people, so we made them readily available for you to seek out, if you need them, and the narrative tells most of the story in a more direct but less specific way.

We have organized the discussion of results around eleven general topics, according to the way the data related to those topics, but the specific findings of the study have been placed just before the tables in the appendices, as described above, for easy reference and cross checking the specific results. However, the discussion of murder in relation to race in America emerged as a new theme as we worked our way through the various analyses, and that discussion occupies four chapters at the end of the book. In some ways, these chapters have become the major focus of this report.

We sensed the relationship of race with murder in our first report, *Violence in America*, but it emerged again—more strongly, this time—and we have elaborated on our original ideas at some length. We recognize that some persons may be "put off" or even offended by these ideas, but we have attempted to explore this problem area with thoughtfulness and sensitivity. We did not feel free to ignore the factual realities that emerged. We hope that the "hypothesis" set forth in Chapter 3 will be useful in thinking about the enigma that exists in our society, and speed all of us on our way to a meaningful and helpful resolution of a terribly difficult cultural problem.

We are indebted to many persons for their assistance on this project: our wives, our colleagues, and specialists in various areas with whom we consulted. Some have helped us through encouragement and recognition for what we have done. Others have helped by raising questions about particular techniques or by challenging inferences we made about what the data mean. To all, we express our grateful thanks.

Jack Frymier

Arliss Roaden

October 2004

Chapter 1
Conclusions: A Place to Begin

People who live in states with low murder rates in the United States live better lives than those who live in states with high murder rates.

They live longer lives, die less frequently from cardiovascular diseases, die less frequently from pneumonia, die less frequently from malignancies, have lower infant mortality rates, die less frequently from accidents, have fewer deaths of pedestrians, they have reduced death rates from highway accidents more, have graduated from high school more frequently, have graduated from college more frequently, read more library books, spend more money per pupil in average daily attendance at public schools, commit fewer murders, commit fewer assaults, commit fewer assaults with guns, commit fewer robberies with guns, commit fewer burglaries, commit fewer larcenies, send fewer persons to prison, spend more on persons who are sent to prison, spend more on judicial processes involving crimes, spend more on police protection, have lower percent black persons in the population, are less promiscuous, have fewer children born with low birth weights, have fewer teenagers who lack health insurance, have fewer teenagers who give birth with inadequate prenatal care, have lower rates of gonorrhea among teenagers, have fewer repeat births among teenagers, vote more frequently in presidential elections, have fewer adults who live below the poverty line, have fewer children who live below the poverty line, provide higher weekly benefits to the unemployed, have fewer bankruptcies, have more households with computers, have fewer persons who smoke cigarettes, have fewer syphilis cases per population, have fewer tuberculosis cases per population, have higher gasoline taxes with which to maintain highways, and get more money from the federal government with which to maintain and improve highways.

Those who live in states that have low murder rates live longer lives and somewhat better lives than those who live in states that have high murder rates, even though in many areas these two groups of states are comparable. The facts are indisputable.

We will repeat these conclusions in chapter 3, but for now, what we have concluded from a study of the 50 states seems to be the place to begin a detailed description of that study: how states with high murder rates differ from states with low murder rates. Later we will describe the similarities.

The Problem of Murder in America

Americans are wonderful people, and they have many positive attributes. But some have negative qualities, too. Occasionally people from other countries call us arrogant, for example, and some of us are. Eric Hoffer, an American longshoreman who became a writer, might have said that some of us are dogmatically convinced of the justness of our cause.[1] "True believers" is what he called such persons. They *know* what is good and true. If those from other nations want to throw verbal stones at us, all right, but if they throw real stones— or even if we think they may throw real stones—that is a different story.

Some of us are absolutely convinced that our way of life, our government, and our economic system are the best in the world, and our purposes are just and noble, even righteous, in a way. Such persons think that Americans are not like those non-believers in other countries. Our traditions and our history prove that we really are better people than those who live in other places and criticize our way. We know!

Asked to explain why our murder rate is almost eight times as high as those who live in Great Britain, say, or France, we attribute such differences to our early history, or even argue that the differences are not that great. "Those other people must not keep good records," some smugly say.

This is a book about murder in America. We intend to report the facts. Not just facts about murder, although we will report those, too, but about various aspects of our culture that may be related to murder that do exist—as cause or consequence—and try to understand what we are really like, as a people. This book is an attempt to help us understand ourselves and our motives better. Maybe we already know just who we are and what we are like. Or maybe we have described ourselves to ourselves with pious platitudes and generalities so often that we have come to believe that we really do know what we are like and what our motives are.

We would like to think that we are raising questions about America because we love it. That is what the publishers of *Harper's Magazine* wrote when Bernard De Voto, who was editor of that great magazine, died almost fifty years ago. Like De Voto, we want America to be better. That is why we raise questions about some things we see and know.

Our approach in these pages will be very simple. We have a lot of information about each of the 50 states in the United States. This information is primarily numerical in nature. We realize that many readers are less comfortable with numbers than they are with words, but numbers tell us something about ourselves in different ways than words. As John Hersey wrote many years ago, words are always ambiguous, while numbers aim at precision.[2] The beauty and power of words inheres in shades of meaning implicit in differing definitions and interpretations available for almost every word in the language. The very purpose of numbers is to dissolve differences and imbue exactness that will enable us to have a richer, fuller understanding of phenomena with which we are concerned. When we try to use numbers to bring precision to things of beauty, sometimes we err, but if we use only words to describe realities that have been defined with numbers, we may err, too.

It is difficult to talk about history in purely numerical ways, for example, but it is equally difficult to talk about economics or physics in purely verbal ways. Our attempt here will be to use both words and numbers to help us understand, and to help you understand.

When a murder occurs, for example, when one human being kills another human being, that incidence of murder is often described exclusively in verbal terms. Newspaper articles and "whodunit" detective stories rely on words to accomplish their purpose. And words accomplish those purposes well. But newspaper articles and detective stories always deal with one murder at a time. They treat murder as an instance of human behavior. They do not conceptualize murder as a category, except for the label, nor do they generalize in ways that would enable us to learn more about murders as a particular type of human activity or why murders take place at all.

Our purpose here will be to use "murder" as a category or type of human conduct that we think is abominable. We could learn a lot by studying or examining one murder in detail, but we can learn something different, and perhaps more helpful to those of us who are not detectives, by studying a hundred or a thousand murders in relation to culture in general and culture in detail.

Murders are intentional. When one person deliberately kills another person, that is first degree murder; an intentional act. There are other categories of homicide—second degree murder, manslaughter—but the label of "murder" implies that the death, if not premeditated, was always a possibility because the perpetrator carried a gun to facilitate a planned robbery, for example, and ended up using the gun for his or her own "protection," and killing another person in the process. Highway deaths, on the other hand, are almost always accidental; they are not planned. Intentionality is an important aspect of any murder trial, because it is the root concept in determining motive.

Three major categories of death—natural, intentional, and accidental—are important because they differentiate causes. In studying the relationship of murder to hundreds of variables at work in society, we are looking for clues regarding cause: what conditions contribute to behaviors that lead one person to kill another person? If we were trying to comprehend conditions that contribute to death on the highway, for example, we would be interested in such factors as road conditions, weather, visibility, and the like. Accidents are often the result of factors beyond human control. Murders, on the other hand, are almost always the result of factors directly under human control.

In murder cases, for example, police are always concerned with the question: "What was the motive?" Motives are important in understanding one murder in particular. Motives are also important in understanding learning in art or mathematics or science. Some children get interested in a particular person in history or an author in literature or a topic in biology, for instance, and those interests often develop into a broader interest in learning in general: a general "motivation to learn," if you please.

In the same way, general motives are important to understand behaviors such as murder as a category or type of human behavior. Why does murder occur more frequently in some states than others? What characterizes those states that have higher murder rates than others? Are people in some states more inclined to aggressive behavior and physical attacks on other persons than people in other areas? Is it something in their diet or genetic background or teachings from parents and others that causes such behaviors to occur more frequently than those that occur in other states? Do people in some states tolerate—or even encourage—behavior that may lead to violence against other people? How do concepts such as "defiance" and "unkindness" and "bullying" relate to murder? These are the kinds of questions that interest us. These are the kinds of questions that we will examine in this study.

Most of the information we have collected in recent years is pegged specifically to states, and that is the information we will use in this particularly inquiry. Some states may "hang together" regionally or comprise a section of the country, but our focus will be on states. That was the way our nation was founded. That is the way our information is available.

States differ: economically, politically, socially, educationally, and in other ways. But more important—or perhaps because they differ—there are significant variations in many aspects of the cultures of various states: death rates from particular causes, health care, crime rates, police protection, incarceration rates, disease rates, tax rates, personal income, educational achievement, creative accomplishments, problems of teenagers, and on and on.

The basic question facing us is this: What are states that are characterized as "high murder rate states" really like? Are the behaviors and beliefs of people who live in those states comparable to those who live in "low murder rate states," or are their behaviors and beliefs different from those who live elsewhere?

We are all Americans. We are free to move about the country. We can express ourselves in speech or writing or otherwise, and we can worship as we please. We are free to make the most or make the least of our talents, abilities, and interests: at home, at work, at school, or play. We are free to partake of our culture in almost any way we please. All of us are governed according to the Constitution of the United States, but we are citizens of only one of 50 states.

Each of those 50 states has its own constitution, and each state is empowered by the federal Constitution to govern those within its territorial limits according to its own stipulated constitution and laws, as long as that constitution and laws do not conflict with the Constitution and laws of the United States. Since the Tenth Amendment to the United States Constitution says that "the powers not delegated to the United States by the Constitution, nor prohibited by it to the States, are reserved to the States respectively, or to the people," each state has latitude over many areas of human activity—crime, education, health, marriage, and voting—to name a few.

Both of us have spent most of our adult lives as educators—teachers, administrators, researchers—in public schools and universities. We have always thought of ourselves as public servants. And we are collectors. We collect information and data about those of us who call ourselves "Americans," including where we live and what we do.

Last year we published *Cultures of the States: A Handbook on Effectiveness of State Governments,*[3] which included data on more than 700 variables for each of the 50 states, plus a profile of each state based on statistical factors over which state governments have control. We developed profiles that showed precisely where each state stood in relation to all of the other states on fifteen factors that were comprised of statistical data from 120 variables that pertained to each of the 50 states. One of the things that "jumped out at us" from that study was how states in the South seemed to cluster together on many of the variables included in that study. Further, when we analyzed those data in detail, we were amazed at how accomplishments in education (e.g., high school graduation and college graduation) correlated with hundreds of other variables for which we had data, and where southern states stood on those variables in relation to other states.

We began this present project with the intention of looking carefully at how states that have more instances of murder compared with other states on matters related to education, but that focus quickly broadened to a more comprehensive perspective: What are the high murder rate states really like? How might such states be characterized with accuracy and precision? What are their strengths? What are their weaknesses? What problems are unique to those states? How do those problems manifest themselves? What contributed to the development of those problems over the years? How are states with high murder rates like the rest of the United States? How are they different?

We know, for example, that some who live in America are legal citizens of particular states, but others are present illegally and only residents of states. Some are rich and some are poor. Some are young and some are old. Some are black, some are white, and some are of other ethnic or racial backgrounds. We have collected information about all those who live and work and play and die in this great country, and we have recorded that information according to the various states in which the people live. We currently have more than a thousand variables for which we have statistical information regarding specific aspects of living and working and playing and dying for each of the 50 states. That information is organized in a database on our computers, and we "play with those data" every day, trying to "make sense of" and "to understand" our people and our country and our states.

We are proud of some of the things we do as a people, but we are appalled and ashamed of other things we do. The United States is a great nation, and we have developed ways to enable our people to do many wonderful things. But we have a sordid record in certain areas, too. Our murder rate is one of the highest in the world. That ought not be. Our health care system is not the best in the world, and it could be and should be the best, given our capabilities and our resources. We have bungled our way into a social and political morass that seems rooted in ideologies and pathologies of thought that prevent us from accomplishing what might otherwise be reasonable objectives to achieve.

It is from this perspective that we elected to analyze and review our data about behavior and conduct of people in states that have high rates of murder, and to compare them with people in the other states. We are not interested in "giving praise" or "finding fault." We want to comprehend, to understand. We want "to know" what the states with high murder rates are really like; how their people live and work and die. We intend to look at those states from a distance and through a numerical lens, and though what we describe will undoubtedly be different from Tom Wolfe's perspective or Samuel Huntington's, we hope it will be useful and accurate, too.

This is a book that is rooted in numbers. We compared two groups of states—one group was defined as having high murder rates, and the other was defined as having lower murder rates—on more than 470 variables for which we had per capita or percent information. We also developed verbal descriptions of what these comparisons meant. The numbers are generally separated from the words, but they are available nearby, if you want to check them.

We realize that most people are more comfortable and more skilled with words than they are with numbers, as we said before, but numbers are important, too. The ambiguities that inhere in words, for instance, are essential. They help us to broaden and deepen our understanding of complex realities involved in life. But numbers bring precision, validity, and expansion to our notions about life and death and work and learning. They also help us to understand, to comprehend, to know. And that is our goal: to know.

As a people, we seem to be making steady progress in our efforts to reduce highway death rates in the United States, but we are not making as much progress in our efforts to reduce murder rates.

For example, there have been more than a million murders in the United States since 1900, [1] and the murder rate was reasonably stable during most of the past century. More people were murdered between 1960 and 2000 (i.e., about 700,000 persons), in fact, than were killed in all of the wars in which the United States was involved from 1898 to the present time.[4]

Statistics about homicides were probably not collected uniformly across all of the states before the 1930s, from all reports, and murder rates have fluctuated in cycles since the time of the Great Depression, but it hard to make a case that murder rates have gone down much during that period and stayed down. More people died from automobile accidents every year since 1930 than died from murder,[5] so there is little doubt that highway fatalities are a bigger killer than homicides, but the rate of death from automobile accidents has gone down steadily over time, even though there are more cars and more people. That is not true in the case of murder.

Identifying States with High Murder Rates and States with Low Murder Rates

Our purpose here was to answer one question: "What are states that have high murder rates really like?" Or, to pose that question in a slightly different way: "How might those states be characterized?" We were not interested in the geography or geology of these states, but in what the people are like? What do they value? How important is life? How important is health? How important is learning? What kinds of laws do the people propose or oppose? What kinds of people do they elect to govern themselves? How deeply involved and committed are they to the idea of "self government?" What kinds of children do they raise? How might those children be described? And on and on. The basic question was: "What are people in states with high murder rates really like?"

To answer that question, we first had to determine which states had high murder rates. We used a simple definition based on one factor: death rates from murder over a 39-year period. "Murder" is a term that people apply to events in which one human being kills another human being. Everybody knows what "murder" means.

If we study the data available on the variable, "MURDER39," which represents the average murder rate in each of the 50 states over a 39-year period, 1960 to 1998, and if we identify states that have "high" murder rates, we can reasonably assume that murder was more frequent and is a more severe problem in those states than in states that do not have "high" murder rates.

Accordingly, we examined one table (i.e., G.268) from the *Cultures* book, [6] described earlier. That table has been reproduced for your convenience in following our thought processes. The data represent the average number of murders per 100,000 population for each state over a 39-year period: 1960 to 1998. Table G.267, which shows the total number of murders in each state for that same 39-year period, is also included to give perspective.

Table G.268, on the next page, depicts the "Average Murder Rate per 100,000 Population Over 39 Years, 1960 to 1998." The data are rank-ordered from high to low on murder rates over a 39-year period. The 25 states in the top half of that distributions are listed below. These 25 states had high murder rates over an extended period of time:

Alabama	Alaska	Arizona	Arkansas	California
Florida	Georgia	Indiana	Illinois	Kentucky
Louisiana	Maryland	Mississippi	Michigan	Missouri
Nevada	New Mexico	New York	North Carolina	Ohio
Oklahoma	South Carolina	Tennessee	Texas	Virginia

In our judgment, the people in these 25 states exhibited less concern for human life as reflected in the data for the criterion variable (i.e., murder rate 1960 to 1998) than was reflected in the data for the other 25 states, which evidenced lower murder rates. From this point forward, when we say "high murder rate states" or "states with high murder rates," we refer to the 25 states listed above. When we say "low murder rate states" or "states with low murder rates" we mean those states below the mid-point on Table 268 which, together with the "high murder rate states," comprise the United States of America.

Table G.268		Table G.267	
MURDER39	STATE	MURD39	STATE
13.20	Louisiana	89,621	California
12.29	Georgia	64,727	Texas
11.68	Alabama	61,447	New York
11.64	Texas	39,557	Florida
11.63	Mississippi	39,454	Illinois
11.34	Nevada	31,507	Michigan
11.17	South Carolina	25,888	Georgia
10.79	Florida	24,493	Ohio
10.04	Alaska	24,253	Pennsylvania
10.04	New York	22,496	North Carolina
9.90	North Carolina	20,953	Louisiana
9.54	Tennessee	17,840	Virginia
9.41	Maryland	17,200	Alabama
9.41	New Mexico	16,628	Tennessee
9.15	California	16,389	Missouri
9.03	Arkansas	15,818	Maryland
8.94	Illinois	14,632	Mew Jersey
8.87	Michigan	13,080	South Carolina
8.66	Virginia	12,937	Indiana
8.55	Missouri	11,188	Mississippi
7.83	Kentucky	10,641	Kentucky
7.77	Arizona	8,489	Arizona
7.29	Oklahoma	8,378	Oklahoma
6.12	Indiana	7,725	Arkansas
5.85	Ohio	7,318	Massachusetts
5.75	Delaware	6,905	Washington
5.70	Colorado	6,234	Colorado
5.40	West Virginia	5,392	Wisconsin
5.24	Pennsylvania	4,824	New Mexico
5.06	New Jersey	4,666	Connecticut
5.03	Wyoming	4,555	Kansas
4.88	Kansas	4,167	Oregon
4.41	Hawaii	3,884	West Virginia
4.24	Oregon	3.797	Minnesota
4.21	Washington	3,740	Nevada
3.82	Connecticut	2,056	Iowa
3.67	Montana	1,825	Nebraska
3.44	Idaho	1,661	Utah
3.25	Massachusetts	1,628	Hawaii
3.00	Nebraska	1,603	Alaska
2.98	Rhode Island	1,311	Delaware
2.93	Utah	1,206	Idaho
2.93	Wisconsin	1,120	Rhode Island
2.35	Minnesota	1,110	Montana
2.23	Maine	967	Maine
2.15	New Hampshire	808	Wyoming
2.11	Vermont	757	New Hampshire
2.09	South Dakota	566	South Dakota
1.85	Iowa	418	Vermont
1.16	North Dakota	293	North Dakota

Comparing "High Murder Rate States" and "Low Murder Rate States"

Having determined which states make up what we call "high murder rate states," we then decided that an appropriate way to look at those states, in comparison with the "low murder rate states," was to test the statistical significance of the difference of mean scores of the two groups of states on hundreds of variables for which we have statistical information. We thought that comparing these two groups of states would be both appropriate and helpful.

Following this rationale, we separated the "high murder rate states" from the "low murder rate states," and compared the two groups on almost every variable for which we had data with which to make comparisons (i.e., almost 475 variables). We used the "t" statistic to test the statistical significance of the difference of mean scores for each variable included in our data base for which such a test was appropriate. We did not employ the "t" statistic to determine whether "total taxes paid to the federal government" differed for the two groups of states, for example, but we did compute "per capita taxes paid to the federal government," and determined the statistical significance of the difference of mean scores of the two groups of states on that variable. We followed that logic throughout the analyses.

We might have used other statistical procedures: analysis of variance, multiple regression, or correlation, for example. We assumed, however, that "t" test would be reasonably understandable by non-statisticians (i.e., most people can understand that mean scores of two groups provide important information regarding differences between those groups). Where the differences are not statistically significant, that will be comprehensible, too.

In the analyses that follow, then, remember these things. First, we collected statistical data on several hundred variables for each of the 50 states. Almost all of this information came from government sources (e.g., Bureau of the Census, Department of Justice, Centers for Disease Control, National Center for Health Statistics, Bureau of Economic Analysis), though some data were provided by agencies such as the Annie E. Casey Foundation, which were also considered reliable. Second, all data that were not already in per capita or percent format were converted to such form by calculation (e.g., dividing the numerical total for a state on a variable by the population of that state). Third, mean scores for the two groups of states (i.e., 25 "high murder rate states" and 25 "low murder rate states") were computed, along with standard deviations for each group, and the "t" statistic was calculated. Fourth, if the "t" value exceeded a stipulated figure (i.e., "t" equal to or greater than plus or minus 1.96 is generally considered significant statistically), it was assumed that the difference between mean scores of the two groups was significant statistically. Fifth, we organized all of this information into various tables in which comparable data were included, and all of those tables are included in this report. Sixth, we summarized the analyses by preparing verbal descriptions of the comparisons, then organized those descriptions into sections of related information (e.g., a section on voting, a section on crime, a section on taxes, and a section on death rates by cause).

Where these two groups of states differed statistically on any of hundreds of comparisons made, such distinctions helped to define the "edges" of those distinctions in empirical ways. Those "edges" highlighted the differences identified and helped us to become aware of and to comprehend the detailed distinctions between both groups of states in various ways. And remember: we do not intend to be critical or judgmental when we use the phrase "high murder rate states" or "low murder rate states." We intend to be descriptive. Our words will be based on valid numbers regarding hundreds of variables, separated on the basis of murder rates from 1960 to 1998, which characterizes the two groups of states that we compared.

Suppose we begin by noting the population of these two groups of states. Slightly more than 200 million people live in the 25 "high murder rate states." Approximately 75 million people live in the 25 "low murder rate states." When we ask, "what are the high murder rate states really like?" we are talking about a lot of people. Yet there was almost no statistical difference in the population density or metropolitan populations of these two groups of states. Many, probably most of the 200 million people who call those 25 states home do not think of their home states as more violent than the other states, and that raises an issue that ought to be discussed: how much is too much?

We are sensitive to the fact that our criteria for defining "high murder rate states" are reasonable, in a technical sense, but they may be unbelievable to those who live in these 25 states. That is because, as horrible as murder is, it is still an infrequent incident in any state. There were 541 murders in Louisiana, for example, the most violent state in that category in 1998, and there were 190 murders that year in Wisconsin. But the Wisconsin population in 1998 was almost five and one quarter million people, and Louisiana's population was just over four million persons. The murder rate in Louisiana, in fact, was almost four times the murder rate in Wisconsin. Why such a huge difference?

We review these examples to underscore a point of which all of us are aware: Murder is not "typical" behavior anywhere. Murder is infrequent in every state. Violence in any form is the stuff we read about in newspapers and watch on television—precisely because it is not typical.

But death is the great equalizer among human beings everywhere. Having said that, it makes no sense at all to ignore death anywhere, and death rates will be an important perspective in this study, because states and state governments have a lot of say about factors that affect life itself.

Our guess is that states which evidence "more violence" in higher murder rates will have higher death rates in natural death—heart disease, cancer, diabeties—and from suicides and accidents, and deaths from other causes. We did not know for sure when we began this study whether there would be differences in natural and accidental death rates between states that evidence "high murder rates" and "low murder rates," as we have defined those terms, but we are convinced that different states have different cultures, and different cultures manifest themselves in terms of people and governments attributing varying importance to things such as living, learning, working, dying, earning, playing, and the like. The real "stuff of life!"

State governments make a difference—for better, or for worse—when it comes to both the quality of life and the quantity of life, however those phrases are defined. We hypothesize that the criterion measure used to separate the 50 states into two groups of 25 states for purposes of comparison—murder rate over 39 years—will separate these two groups so sharply there will be discernible and significant differences in other aspects of human existence. Culture is an extremely powerful force—for human betterment or for human degradation—and we are certain that much of the shaping power of culture is rooted in and manifest through state government.

What we will examine in forthcoming pages will be the consequences of what state governments have done over time: How much money they collected in taxes, and how they spent the moneys collected. How supportive or how vindictive they were in enacting and enforcing laws defining crime and misconduct. How supportive or how miserly they were regarding health care for the elderly, education for the young, highways for commerce, insurance for the unemployed, and the like. We intend to look at hundreds of instances of human behavior within the confines of each of the 50 states that have generated data and information that are available for all to see. In addition, we will tell you where that information is and how to find it, so you can verify (or try to refute) the information base that we will analyze.

Finally, we analyzed the data, studied the analyses, and made inferences about the two groups of states examined with precision in various ways. And we drew conclusions.

Chapter 2 describes, in general terms, the relationship of high murder rates to hundreds of facets of life in America in high murder rate and low murder rate states. The details of those relationships are set forth in Appendices A through K, where specific findings are itemized for each of eleven broad categories (e.g., voting, taxes, crime, health care), and the statistical comparisons are presented in 40 separate tables. The first section of Chapter 2 provides information about how to go through the findings and statistical comparisons.

Chapter 2
The Correlates of Murder

At this point we intend to overview the chapters and appendices that follow to help you make sense of all the numbers there, but first a bit of review. We collected data on hundreds of variables from reliable sources over a period of many months. Most of the data were published in 2003 in *Cultures of the States: A Handbook on Effectiveness of State Governments,*[1] but some were collected from the internet since that book was published. Following separation of the fifty states into two groups—25 states with high murder rates and 25 states with low murder rates—we compared the two groups of states on approximately 475 variables thought to relate to areas affected by state government with the "t" test to determine the statistical significance of the difference between mean scores of the two groups of states on each of those variables.

How to Interpret the Results

In the sections that follow, a brief discussion of findings is presented, organized around topics such as "voting," "taxation," or "crime, punishment, and police protection." A listing of all of the findings and detailed analyses of all of the data are included in appended materials later in the book, organized around these same topics. To help you comprehend and "make sense" of the detailed information presented later, we will outline here how the tabular information that is presented is organized. You may want to turn to a particular appendix to study the findings and statistical comparisons before you move on to the next topic.

Described on the next page is part of Table 12, including two "lines" of information and data, plus the table headings, copied from that table, in Appendix C that follows. Both lines refer to one comparison. The first line presents statistical information on one variable, and it is in the upper half of the page. The second line defines the variable on which the two groups of states were compared, and it is generally in the lower half of the page. Remember that each "line" in a table represents one variable, and the data regarding how that information pertains to each of the two groups of states that we are comparing: "high murder rate states" and "low murder rate states." To help you follow the discussion more carefully, we have put this partial illustration of a total table from one of the appendices on the next page, and discussion of particular aspects of that table, on the following page. All of this is intended to help those less experienced in reading this kind of statistical information.

The numbers in this book are important—the heart of the entire project—and you need a solid understanding of how the tables have been put together, and how to make sense of the details that are there.

Example from Table 12

Comparison of Mean Values for Food Costs per Inmate per Day
in 25 High Murder Rate States and 25 Low Murder Rate States with the "t" Statistic

Variables	Table	25 High Murder States Mean	25 Low Murder States Mean	25 High States SD	25 Low States SD	"t" value
FOODPI	G.70	2.67	3.67	1.09	.97	- 3.404 **

FOODPI	=	Food costs per inmate, per day				1996

First, note that the title of this particular table is a summary or abstract of the information included in the table: a "comparison of mean values for the food costs per inmate per day in 25 high murder rate states and 25 low murder rate states with the "t" statistic."

The column labels depicts what is found beneath each heading. Note that the variable on which the two groups of states were compared was "FOODPI," the mean food costs per inmate per day incarcerated in the prisons in each of the various states. The G.70 under "Table" indicates that the numerical values reported were obtained from Table G.70 in Appendix G of the *Cultures of the States* book, cited earlier in this chapter. If there had been three asterisks in that space instead of G.70, (i.e., " *** "), a reference at the bottom of the page would have indicated the internet address where that information had been obtained from the internet since the *Cultures* book was published. The second "FOODPI" line defines that variable as "food costs per inmate, per day" for the year 1996. When you look at the actual tables in the appendices that follow, most of this will make sense.

The mean value for the 25 high murder rate states was $2.67 per prisoner in those states, and the mean value for the 25 low murder rate states was $3.67 per prisoner in those states. Next, note that SD (i.e., standard deviation, a statistic necessary to compute "t" values for comparing mean scores) was 1.09 for high murder rate states and .97 for low murder rate states. Standard deviation reflects the variance within each group; the "spread" of scores involved.

The "t" statistic at the far right side of the table is reported as " - 3.404 ** " which shows three things: the "-" sign indicates that the second group listed on the line had the highest mean value (i.e., $3.67 as compared to $2.67). If there had been no minus sign, that would have meant that the first group listed had the highest mean. Second, the "3.404" number is the "t" value itself, to be compared with a table of "t" values which shows whether that number is large enough to suggest "statistical significance." Recall that we said earlier in this chapter that any "t" value of "plus or minus 1.96 or larger" indicates that the two mean scores differed at a level of "statistical significance." The "3.404" clearly exceeds the "plus or minus 1.96" level described. Third, the two asterisks (i.e., " ** ") following the "3.404" indicate that the difference was large enough for the reader to assume that "the difference between the mean scores compared was statistically significant at or beyond a .01 level of confidence." Such a level of confidence means that readers may assume that such a difference would have occurred less than once by chance in a hundred comparisons, and this is probably not the time to assume that chance was involved. Larger "t" values indicate less likelihood that such differences might have occurred by chance. In other words, there is probably some explanation which is better than "chance" that these differences are real: they may have been caused.

In this whole project we compared almost 500 differences between mean scores of the two groups of states being studied. We could expect that, at the .01 level of confidence, five or so such comparisons might have resulted in a "t" value this large by chance (i.e., 1 percent of 500 comparisons made would suggest that five such comparisons might have occurred by chance). Or, if one asterisk (i.e., *) is reported, that would mean that the "t" value was "at or beyond the .05 level of confidence."

Finally, to determine "similarity" or "no difference," as opposed to a "statistically significant difference" between the groups of states, we will use a "rule of thumb" that is not typically used in statistical analyses. We will assume that, if the "t" value is less than 1.000, the groups are similar or comparable. If the "t" value is 1.96 or larger, the groups differ at a statistically significant level.

In the appendices that follow, all of the analyses are preceded by terse statements of findings: what the analyses show. Then the analyses are presented—about 10 or 12 comparisons in a table on each page—in the layout, described above, to help you know how to make sense of the thousands of numbers that follow. Wherever possible, we grouped statistical comparisons on the same topic (e.g., death, taxes, income, teenager's problems) together. These groupings are not perfect, but they expedite the reading process.

Murder and Voting

The data comparing 25 high murder rate states with 25 low murder rate states on persons registered to vote in presidential elections from 1960 to 2000 (see Appendix A) are both consistent and clear: more people in low murder rate states registered to vote, and seven of the eleven differences were significant statistically. And in every presidential election since 1960, more persons from low murder rate states actually voted than persons from high murder rate states, and every one of the eleven comparisons was significant statistically.

In the 25 high murder rate states, percentages of those who voted in the elections ranged from 47.75 percent to 56.02 percent during that 40 year period. In the 25 low murder rate states, voting participation ranged from 56.84 percent to a high of 73.10 percent. In general (except for the 1992 election), however, percentages of those from low murder rate states who actually voted tended to decrease steadily from 1960 to 1996, even though significantly more persons from low murder rate states voted in every one of the elections between 1960 to 2000 than persons from high murder rate states. It is important to note, though, that the range of differences narrowed considerably between the two groups of states during that 40-year period. Why that range steadily narrowed over the years was not apparent to us.

Proportionately more persons from low murder rate states voted than persons from high murder rate states in every presidential election from 1960 to 2000. People who live in low murder rate states evidenced better citizenship behaviors in regards to voting than people who live in high murder rate states, and the differences were significant statistically.

Murder and Taxes

States collect taxes and states expend taxes. In addition, states receive money from the federal government for various specified purposes (e.g., highway construction, education, health care). Tax collections at the state level are based on such things as property, income, and sales. Tax expenditures are based on categories such as highways, prisons, Medicaid, and education.

Information regarding tax collections and tax expenditures came from various sources. The Bureau of Economic Analysis provides detailed information about taxes collected by the federal government, state governments, and local governments. Information regarding tax expenditures came from the National Association of State Budget Officers. Information from both sources is provided in the form of total dollars, percent, and per capita figures.

To compare states on a particular taxation factor, sometimes it was necessary to divide total dollar figures by the states' population for a given year to determine per capita values for that year, whether the concern was about collections or expenditures. And sometimes the traditions involved in reporting made it difficult to make valid comparisons of states on certain areas, because the need for precise reporting has not arisen in certain areas of governmental activity as frequently as it has in others. For instance, providing information about funds expended per student in public schools has been used by states for more than half a century. Providing information about funds expended by a state per inmate in prison or per mile of highway constructed is of more recent origin.

What is obvious from the taxation tables (see Appendix B) is that high murder rate states collected slightly less money at the state and local levels in taxes, and low murder rate states collected slightly more money, but none of those differences were significant statistically. What is not obvious is whether those minor differences are a function of economics or philosophy. Table 5 suggests that the tax rates of the two groups of states differ less than one half of one percent per capita population.

Of the 81 comparisons of mean scores of high murder rate states with low murder rate states, only one of those 81 comparisons was significantly different, and in that instance, people who lived in high murder rate states paid more money in taxes than people who lived in low murder rate states. For every one of the comparisons that did not differ at a level of statistical significance, the differences were such that slightly higher taxes were paid by persons who lived in low murder rate states, but none of the differences compared were significant statistically.

Murder, Crime, Punishment, and Police Protection

Table 10 presents information about seven crime rates for the year 1998, and it also presents information about those same seven crimes for the 39-year period 1960 to 1998 (see Appendix C). Murder, assault, rape, robbery, burglary, and car theft rates for high murder rate states and low murder rate states differed significantly for 1998, and five of those same crime rates differed significantly over the 39-year period. In every comparison made, and in every instance in which comparisons differed at a statistically significant level, high murder rate states had higher mean scores for crime, and low murder rate states had lower mean scores. Murder is a violent crime, and it is clearly related to other types of crime.

Table 11 presents information along the same line as that presented in Table 10: crime rates of various types. In two areas—percent of all robberies that were fist related, and percent of all assaults that were fist related—average crime rates were significantly higher in low murder rate states than in high murder rate states. In terms of robberies per 100,000 population, percent of robberies with a gun, assaults per 100,000 population, percent of assaults with a gun, number of murders per person in local government, and number of crimes per person in the state, however, statistics all indicate higher crime rates for persons who live in the 25 high murder rate states. It is interesting that the two categories in which significantly higher crime rates occurred in the 25 low murder rate states were both characterized as "fist related" rather than "gun related," fists being less lethal than guns. In other words, even when the statistics "go the other way," less violent measures were employed.

Look now, for a moment, at Tables 12, 13, and 14: expenditures for corrections and justice variables. What is immediately apparent is that 27 of the 40 comparisons of mean values for expenditures differed at a level that was statistically significant. Almost all of the information about crime presented thus far suggests that high murder rate states have a higher incidence of crime, and there is clear evidence that high murder rate states are spending more for corrections than low murder rate states. States with low murder rates tend to spend more for police protection and judicial processes.

Go back now to Table 12 in Appendix C. Note that PRISPI96, "operating costs per inmate, per year," reflects significantly different values expended for incarcerating prisoners for states with high murder rates and states with low murder rates for 1996, with states with low murder rates spending, on average, almost 50 percent more per inmate in their prisons than states with high murder rates that year. This information was generated by an independent researcher in a way that compared "costs per inmate per year" (see Table G.67 in *Cultures*). Minnesota, Rhode Island, Maine, Alaska, Utah, Connecticut, and Oregon spent almost four times as much per inmate as Alabama spent, though Alaska is one of the high murder rate states.

The variables MEDICI, FOODPI, and UTILPIPD variables are all defined in "per inmate" ways: medical care per inmate per day, food costs per inmate per day, and utilities costs per inmate per day. Each of these variables reflect statistically significant differences between mean scores of the 25 high murder rate states and the 25 low murder rate states, and comparisons indicate that low murder rate states spent more per inmate per day than high murder rate states.

Suppose we take a moment here to try to sharpen the discussion still further. We will begin by stating what may be prevailing assumptions regarding two different public institutions: hospitals and prisons. Hospitals are built to serve the people inside the institution. Prisons are built to serve the people outside the institution. That is the way some people see these things, anyway.

If we accept the assumption that hospitals are built to serve the welfare of the people inside the institution, then it seems both reasonable and important to collect and report data that reflect that basic assumption: how many people die, how many people get well, how much it costs to care for each person, and on and on. States with high crime rates incarcerate more persons than states with low crime rates, thus the total expenditures for prisons are usually higher than expenditures of states with lower crime rates, but expenditures per inmate are lower. That suggests a more vindictive approach to incarceration rather than a supportive approach, yet there also seems to be a clear relationship between higher expenditures per inmate and lower crime rates. This issue is worthy of further examination.

We raise this issue as gently as we can because we do not mean to question the integrity of those who collect taxes and account for expenditures in the areas of crime, punishment, and police protection. We have a feeling, however, that some policymakers may intend (without being fully conscious of it at all) lesser expenditures per inmate for prisons to serve as additional punishment for those who have transgressed: less adequate food, fewer guards, more difficult living conditions, less medical attention, and the like. Our guess is that society is just now becoming more fully aware of how different philosophical assumptions about punishment for crimes may manifest themselves in very different practices and policies in prison operations.

Theoretically, we might posit a continuum as a basis for thinking and talking about prison operations. One end of that continuum might be described as positive and supportive. The other end might be described as negative and vindictive. We are not specialists in corrections or prison operations at all, but we know that such philosophical assumptions permeate many other areas of governmental activity and policy: how to treat and care for homeless people, drug addicts, pedophiles, foster children, unemployed workers, homosexuals, unmarried mothers, AIDS victims, and the like. Sometimes government is helpful, supportive, and positive with members of society who are affected by or afflicted with particular problems. Sometimes government is punitive, vindictive, and negative with members of society who are affected by or afflicted with particular problems.

If you go back and look at the data in Table 12 in Appendix C, for example, it is hard to avoid the inference that states that have the most severe punishments (i.e., number of executions), the lowest expenditures per prisoner for food and medicine, the lowest operating costs per inmate per year, and the lowest expenditures for judicial processes and police protection tend to have the highest crime rates. Are these a direct result of corrections policies? It is terribly difficult to relate financial costs to cause and effect in an area such as crime and corrections, but it is easy to conclude that using prison as punishment (i.e., incarceration as a place to separate prisoners from home and family) is a very different kind of public policy than using prison as a place for additional punishmen (i.e., poor food, limited medical care, poorly paid guards). Issues such as these must be examined carefully and thoughtfully by policymakers.

The question is: are taxpayers the clients, or are prisoners the clients? Policymakers obviously are elected by taxpayers, not prisoners, but the evidence here seems to suggest that what we have called "vindictive" incarceration policies may result in more crime, not less crime, and spending minimal amounts to care for prisoners in the short run may cost taxpayers more in the long run. That does not serve taxpayers well. This problem warrants careful study.

Murder and Demographic Factors

Many factors that would normally be thought of as "demographic" in nature—years of education, income, type of employment, birthrate—have been subsumed under other headings in this project. Of those factors not included elsewhere, only four were found to be significantly different for high murder rate states and low murder rate states: percent majority population, percent minority population, percent of population that was black, and the percent of women firms per female population.

There was no appreciable difference between high murder rate states and low murder rate states on the following factors: percent of population that was classified as metropolitan, child abuse as percent of population, percent of population under the age of 18 or over the age of 65, percent of families that own their own home, number of persons per household, and the percent of children not immunized. See Appendix D for details.

Murder and Death Rates

In comparing death rates from various causes in high murder rate states and low murder rate states, we calculated the statistical significance of difference of mean scores for 75 different variables in our database (see Appendix E). Most of those variables (i.e., 52) were both racial and gender specific. Of the 75 comparisons made of mean death rates between the two groups of states, 36 differed at a level that was statistically significant, and in 34 of those 36 comparisons, death rates were significantly higher in states with high murder rates than in states with low murder rates. The two instances in which death rates were higher for low murder rate states both involved deaths that were drug-induced (i.e., overdose of drugs).

As a category of cause of death, "death from all causes" differed significantly for white women, black women, white men, and black men. "Death from cardiovascular" problems differed significantly for white women, black women, white men, and black men. Likewise, "death from accidents" differed significantly for white women and white men, and for all persons, regardless of race or gender. In the same way, "automobile death rates" differed at a statistically significant level for white women, black women, white men, black men, and for all persons, regardless of race or gender. Homicides also differed significantly for white women and white men, and for the variable which described death by homicide regardless of race or gender, but the relationship of the criterion variable and comparison variables were similar. The consistency of murder rates over time is simply another example of how the cultures of states are fairly stable over time.

When we look at the comparison on variable PCFATCH in Table 23 in Appendix E, we see almost a perfect negative correlation between "percent change in traffic fatalities between 1975 and 1999" and "high murder rate states." One must study Table G.345, as it was published originally in the *Cultures* book, to realize how negative (i.e., increasing fatalities or low percent changes are all listed at the top of table, how positive (i.e., decreasing fatalities or high percent changes) are all listed at the bottom of the table, and how dramatic the differences were—from a 70 percent increase in highway fatalities for Mississippi, to a 52 percent decrease in highway fatalities for Massachusetts—during the quarter of a century for which the change in highway fatality rates were measured.

There were no significant differences in death rates from falls for white women, black women, white men, or black men in high murder rate states or low murder rate states, nor were any differences in death rates attributed to alcohol or failure to use a seat belt identified.

All things considered, natural death rates were significantly higher for high murder rate states than for low murder rate states in many categories of cause of death. It is difficult not to recognize that cultural or governance forces are operating here that cause these differences to be consistent "across the board," and "over time," so to speak. Higher death rates from most natural causes except cancer were the pattern for persons who lived in high murder rate states, when compared with persons who lived in low murder rate states. Higher death rates in general are a defining characteristic of the high murder rate states' culture.

Murder and Teenager's Social Problems

Young people across America encounter social problems of various kinds. In this project, we compared high murder rate states with low murder rate states on 25 variables for which we had information regarding teenager's social problems. Fourteen of those 25 comparisons differed at a level that was significant statistically, and in 11 of those 14 comparisons, teenagers who lived in high murder rate states experienced more problems than those who lived in low murder rate states. See Appendix F for details.

Unmarried teens between the ages of 15 and 19 who lived in high murder rate states had higher birth rates than those who lived in low murder rate states, although Hispanic teens who lived in low murder rate states had higher birth rates than Hispanic teens who lived in high murder rate states. Likewise, teenagers who smoked and also gave birth were significantly more common in low murder rate states.

In general, teenagers who lived in high murder rate states were plagued with problems associated with sex more frequently than teenagers who lived in low murder rate states. For example, birthrates for unmarried females ages 15 to 19 were dramatically higher (i.e., "t" value of 7.905) in high murder rate states than in low murder rate states, significantly more children were born to unmarried teens, more children were born who were low birth weight, more children were born to unmarried females, more children were born who had inadequate prenatal care, and there were more males and females ages 12 to 19 who lacked health insurance who lived in high murder states than in low murder rate states. Gonorrhea rates among females ages 15 to 19 were also much higher in high murder rate states.

There were no significant differences in abortion rates per 1,000 population for females from high murder rate states when compared with females from low murder rate states, and no differences in birth rates for unmarried black teens or Hispanic black teens the same age.

For whatever reasons, teenagers in high murder rate states experienced significantly more problems related to sex than teenagers in low murder rate states.

Murder and Education

Funding public elementary and secondary schools and public colleges and universities is a primary function of state governments in the United States. We compared high murder rate states with low murder rate states on 62 variables related to education in this project, but only six of those statistical comparisons were significantly different.

Significantly more persons over the age of 25 in low murder rate states reported to the Census Bureau that they had graduated from high school than persons in high murder rate states. The same was true for persons who reported that they had graduated from college. Starting salaries for teachers, however, were significantly higher in high murder rate states than in low murder rate states in 1998. Average salaries for teachers were not significantly different.

The per capita expenditures of total funds devoted to public education from 1989 through 1998 indicate that there were no appreciable differences between high murder rate states and low murder rate states in spending for public education or higher education during most of those years, although funding for public schools in 1997 and 1998 were higher for low murder rate states, according to two sources.

Murder, Employment, and Work

The most striking findings in studying the 58 comparison of high murder rate states and low murder rate states on matters related to employment and work (see Appendix H for details) related to personal income. In none of the comparisons accomplished with the "t" test of the statistical significance of difference of mean scores did persons in low murder rate states have higher per capita income, higher per capita disposable income (i.e., after taxes), higher median income, or higher average pay than persons in high murder rate states. A higher percent of workers from low murder rate states were employed in the areas of trade and finance, and there were some differences in unemployment weekly benefits for workers from low murder rate states, but in the areas of temporary assistance and food stamps, workers from high murder rate states fared better than workers from low murder rate states.

In areas related to poverty there were statistically significant differences which indicated that persons from low murder rate states had fewer persons in poverty than high murder rate states, and there were also fewer bankruptcies, more patents obtained, and more computers used in low murder rate states.

Murder, Health Care, and Other Assistance

This chapter does not address the most pressing questions related to health care in America today, and those questions relate to the increases that have occurred in this area during the past decade or so. Dramatic increases in the health care area have absorbed more of the expenditures during that time by state governments than any other area of governmental effort: highways and transportation, prisons and corrections, elementary and secondary education, higher education, and public assistance. Our comparisons here, however, have been between categories of aid at any one time rather than over extended periods of time. There is certainly reason to believe that increases in health care costs over time have negatively affected allocations to highways, prisons, schools, colleges, and public assistance in profound ways, but our comparisons do not account for such changes. Our attention is devoted exclusively to comparisons on a year-to-year basis of differences between high murder rate states and low murder rate states on the major categories of state governmental expenditures described above: highways and transportation, prisons and corrections, K-12 education, post-secondary education, health care, and public assistance. In this chapter we address only the health care and assistance comparisons between the two groups of states. (see Appendix I)

To get some sense of the changes that have occurred over time, however, Figures 1 and 2 below for states which had high or low murder rates shows the percent of expenditures devoted to six of seven major categories to which states allocate funds (figures rounded): Medicaid, elementary and secondary education, higher education, corrections, highways and transportation, and public assistance. There is an additional category that states use—"other"—which we have not shown here, but it is very small, generally, and targeted objectives are not specified.

	1989	1990	1991	1992	1993	1994	1995	1996	1997	1998	1999	2000
Med	10	12	14	17	19	19	18	19	19	19	18	18
K-12	26	25	25	23	22	22	22	22	22	22	22	22
HEd	15	15	15	14	14	14	14	15	15	15	13	15
Corr	3	3	3	3	3	3	4	3	3	4	3	3
Trans	12	11	10	10	10	9	9	9	9	9	9	9
Ass't	3	3	2	3	3	2	2	2	2	1	1	1

Figure 1

Percent of All Expenditures by High Murder Rate States for Six Categories of Funding

Figure 2 below shows the percent of funds devoted to the same categories for states which had low murder rates:

	1989	1990	1991	1992	1993	1994	1995	1996	1997	1998	1999	2000
Med	10	11	12	15	17	17	17	19	18	18	18	18
K-12	20	20	21	20	20	19	20	20	21	21	21	21
HEd	13	12	12	12	11	11	10	11	11	11	11	11
Corr	3	3	3	3	3	3	3	3	3	3	3	3
Trans	12	13	12	12	11	11	11	11	11	11	11	11
Ass't	4	4	4	4	4	4	3	3	3	2	2	2

Figure 2

Percent of All Expenditures by Low Murder Rate States for Six Categories of Funding

If you compare the percent values in Figures 1 and 2 above, note the steady increases in percent of funds devoted to Medicaid over the 12-year period in both tables (i.e., the percent figures almost double), but slight declines or no changes in the percent of funds devoted to the remaining five categories. Medicaid is slowly "consuming" the rest of every state's budget allocations. Every policymaker knows that, and most people have heard about the steadily increasing "chunk" of expenditures that must be devoted to health care costs, but these two figures highlight that reality.

States across the country tend to devote similar proportions of their budget to these six categories; few comparisons of the differences between high murder rate states and low murder rate states were statistically significant.

There were significantly more cases of syphilis, AIDS, and tuberculosis among persons from high murder rate states, and more instances of persons without health insurance, persons who smoked, and persons who were obese from high murder rate states than from low murder rate states, but there were no important differences in the number of physicians or hospital beds available to people in the two groups of states. Dollars for each Medicare enrollee were higher in high murder rate states in 1999, but dollars for each Medicaid recipient were higher in low murder rate states that same year. There were more facilities for treating drug and alcohol abuse in high murder rate states, and a higher percent of clients were in treatment than in low murder rate states, but there were no appreciable differences in spending for such abuse clinics, for cash help provided by the states, or for average Medicaid expenditures over time.

Murder, Highways, and Transportation

Low murder rate states imposed significantly higher gasoline taxes on their residents than high murder rate states, and low murder rate states got significantly higher federal grants, per capita, from the Highway Transportation Fund than high murder rate states. Likewise, low murder rate states had significantly higher per capita expenditures for highways in 1996, but not for other years. (see Appendix J)

Again, we encourage you to study the data in the appendices at the back of this book to get a more comprehensive and more detailed picture of the relationship of murder to the hundreds of variables that we included in this study. The major differences between the two groups of states, statistically, were most apparent in three areas: death rates from most causes, crime rates in general, and in the area of problems experienced by teenagers. States that had high murder rates typically also had higher death rates, higher crime rates, and higher rates of problems experienced by teenagers. We do not know why states with high and low murder rates differed in these particular areas (although the difference in general crime rates seems plausible), but these problems need further study.

Murder and General Factors

When we produced the *Cultures* book, described earlier, we summarized our findings by calculating 15 factors that were predicated on 120 variables. We then plotted the values for each state, using the 15 factor scores, plus a general summary factor score, in such a way that a profile was generated for each of the 50 states (see Appendix B in the *Cultures* book). In this final set of analyses, we compared the high murder rate states with the low murder rate states on each of those 15 factor scores and the one summary factor score (see Appendix K). Higher scores indicate more problems. Lower scores indicate fewer problems.

When we calculated the differences of the two groups of states' mean scores on each of the 16 factors, it was determined that 14 of the 16 comparisons differed at a statistically significant level. States that had higher murder rates over a 39-year period were very different from states that had lower murder rates over a 39-period of time, and the states with higher murder rates had more problems in every category in which the difference was statistically significant. The cultures of these two groups of states are simply different in important ways.

In the next chapter, we will review the findings again that lead to conclusions, then examine an anomaly that emerged in this study: why black Americans kill other Americans more often than any other racial or ethnic group.

Chapter 3
A Tough Question: Is Race a Factor?

General Conclusions

People who live in the 25 states with low murder rates in the United States live better lives than those who live in the 25 states with high murder rates.

They live longer lives, die less frequently from cardiovascular diseases, die less frequently from pneumonia, die less frequently from malignancies, have lower infant mortality rates, die less frequently from accidents, have fewer deaths of pedestrians, they have reduced death rates from highway accidents more, have graduated from high school more frequently, have graduated from college more frequently, read more library books, spend more money per pupil in average daily attendance at public schools, commit fewer murders, commit fewer assaults, commit fewer assaults with guns, commit fewer robberies with guns, commit fewer burglaries, commit fewer larcenies, send fewer persons to prison, spend more on persons who are sent to prison, spend more on judicial processes involving crimes, spend more on police protection, have lower percents of black persons in the population, are less promiscuous, have fewer children born with low birth weights, have fewer teenagers who lack health insurance, have fewer teenagers who give birth with inadequate prenatal care, have lower rates of gonorrhea among teenagers, have fewer repeat births among teenagers, are registered more frequently to vote in presidential elections, vote more frequently in presidential elections, have fewer adults who live below the poverty line, have fewer children who live below the poverty line, provide higher weekly benefits to the unemployed, have fewer bankruptcies, have more households with computers, have fewer persons who smoke cigarettes, have fewer syphilis cases per population, have fewer tuberculosis cases per population, have higher gasoline taxes with which to maintain highways, and get more money from the federal government with which to maintain and improve highways.

Those who live in states that have low murder rates live longer lives and better lives than those who live in states that have high murder rates, even though in many areas these two groups of states are comparable. The facts are indisputable.

Murder Rates for Black Males Are High

One of the findings of this study was that proportionately more blacks live in states with high murder rates than live in states with low murder rates (see Table 16 in Appendix D). When that fact is added to the fact that the number of murders committed by black males is extremely high, it raises a question that cannot be ignored: Is race a factor in the murder equation in the United States? Black males commit more murders than any other race or gender group in the United States. [1] Table 2 below summarizes that fact.

Table 2

Trends in Homicide Offending Rates (per 100,000 Population, males only)

Year	Ages 14-17 White	Black	Ages 18-24 White	Black	Ages 25 + White	Black
1976	7.9	51.2	16.7	138.3	7.2	76.5
1978	7.7	44.4	18.0	131.2	7.5	71.5
1980	8.9	48.9	20.4	144.6	7.9	71.4
1982	8.1	45.7	17.5	120.8	7.6	62.3
1984	6.9	33.4	18.0	91.1	7.0	51.0
1986	9.0	51.0	18.5	117.2	7.1	55.9
1988	9.9	72.6	16.9	146.9	6.4	50.5
1990	14.3	113.8	22.2	200.7	6.6	48.9
1992	14.4	122.5	21.7	219.0	5.5	42.6
1994	15.6	139.6	20.9	201.0	5.3	35.5

The table above provides information about homicides in terms of perpetrators, those who committed murders between 1976 and 1994. Black males of all ages committed six to ten times as many murders, per population, as white males. The differences are staggering. The key statistical findings of the above report are highlighted below:

* From 1985 to 1994, the rate of murder committed by teens, ages 14-17, increased 172 percent. The rate of killing rose sharply for both black and white male teenagers, but not for females.

* Remaining just above one percent of the population, black males ages 14-24 now constitute 17 percent of the victims of homicide and over 30 percent of the perpetrators. Their white counterparts remained about 10 percent of the victims, about 18 percent of the perpetrators, yet declined in proportionate size of the population.

* Guns, and especially handguns, have played a major role in the surge of juvenile murder. Since 1984, the number of juveniles killing with a gun has quadrupled, while the number killing with all other weapons combined has remained virtually constant.

* The largest increase in juvenile homicide involves offenders who are friends and acquaintances of their victims.

* From 1989 to 1994, the arrest rate for violent crimes (murder, rape, robbery and aggravated assault) rose over 46 percent among teenagers, but only about 12 percent among adults. In terms of arrest rates per 100,000 population, 14-17 year-olds have now surpassed young adults, 18-24.

In Table D.10 below, which was copied from the *Cultures* book, referred to earlier, death rates of murder victims are depicted, by gender and race.[2] The data are not directly comparable to the data in the table above, but they provide some basis for comparison.

Table D.10

Comparison of Death Rates in the United States for Homicide, by Gender and Race

Variable	Table Appendix G	States	Mean	SD	"t"
WWHOMICI	G.109	26	2.67	.94	-13.82 **
WBHOMICI	G.110	26	10.54	2.95	
WWHOMICI	G.109	42	2.66	.92	- 9.04 **
MWHOMICI	G.135	42	6.82	3.64	
WWHOMICI	G.109	37	2.73	.94	-17.72 **
MBHOMICI	G.136	37	53.18	17.19	
WBHOMICI	G.110	26	10.54	2.95	4.64 **
MWHOMICI	G.135	26	6.85	2.93	
WBHOMICI	G.110	26	10.54	2.95	-14.37 **
MBHOMICI	G.136	26	54.62	18.15	
MWHOMICI	G.135	37	7.20	3.69	-15.79 **
MBHOMICI	G.136	37	53.18	17.19	

** t-value significant beyond .01 level of confidence

WW = White women
WB = Black women
MW = White men
MB = Black men

The homicide rate of black males reported in Table D.10 was more than twenty times as high as the rate for white females, five times as high as the rate for black females, and more than seven times as high as the rate for white males. Murders of black males is completely "off the charts" in the data reported here.

Taken together, these reports comprise evidence of extremely high murder rates: of blacks, and by blacks. It is not primarily whites who have been killing blacks or blacks who have been killing whites, but blacks have been killing other blacks at unbelievably high rates. Most of these murders took place in large cities, and most (in recent years, at least) have been tied directly to illegal distribution of narcotics and other drugs, [3] the general level of the economy, and the availability of guns. [4] The dramatic differences between murder rates of black persons and white persons, however, are indisputable. Murder rates among blacks are out of control. Race is a clearly a factor in murder in America that must be explained.

Reflecting on this problem, we developed an hypothesis which might be a partial explanation for these extreme differences in murder rates among blacks, when compared with whites in America. In the next section we will sketch a brief explanation of this hypothesis, with historical justifications that make it both plausible and attractive as a possible explanation of the race factor in murder in America. A complete history of blacks in America may be required to understand what causes black citizens to become the kinds of people they are today to explain these extreme differences in murder rates, but we are neither knowledgeable enough nor skilled enough to attempt such an undertaking. A brief review of certain historical factors may be helpful, though.

An Hypothesis and Its Relation to the Culture of Slavery

We were hesitant even to raise the issue of race in our study of murder in America, but two facts and the emerging hypothesis forced us to confront the race factor directly. The facts are these: legislation cannot change an individual's race, and the homicide rate by black males is extremely high. The hypothesis, which has not been demonstrated as fact but seems plausible, is this:

> ***Blacks in early America grew up in a culture of slavery and were acculturated over an extremely long period of time to be dependent (rather than independent) human beings. After emancipation and amendments to the Constitution assuring equality, the intransigence of whites and the refusal of courts to legitimize equality fostered the development of "learned helplessness" on the part of many blacks. Incremental steps by the federal government in the direction of equality in mid-twentieth century eventually led to frustration and then aggression rather than reason and persuasion***

to resolve disagreements. Independent and responsible behavior began to develop throughout the black community toward the end of the twentieth century, following changes in both policies and structures of the federal government, but black males, especially, continue to engage in aberrant behaviors.

Slavery, by definition, means that those subjected are dependent, not independent, and dependence always involves a kind of slavery to someone or something: the plantation owner, drugs, nicotine, alcohol, money, approval, or what not. Dependence means that, in the eye of the dependent person, other people have the power, other people make the decisions, and other people are responsible for what happens. In other words, "I am not accountable because I've had no say in anything." Freedom and independence include the opportunity to exercise personal choice and to learn to be responsible.

If we look at things from a short-term perspective, most of us tend to assume that people can change if they will simply put their minds and hearts into the effort to learn new things. That is certainly true if we are talking about learning facts or concepts or skills. It is not at all true if we are talking about learning to bring about changes in personality, values, or attitudes. Those aspects of human existence develop more slowly and can only be changed over long periods of time, and sometimes not at all.

Psychotherapists know how difficult it is to help people modify aspects of their personality structure: perceptual style, defense mechanisms, conceptions of self and others, beliefs about personal worthiness, and the like. Such attributes, most of which have been shaped by both genetic and experiential factors, are less amenable to deliberate teaching and change efforts than solving quadratic equations, understanding the idea of separation of powers in government, or balancing equations in chemistry. Basic beliefs and personality characteristics are deeply embedded in the human psyche and much more difficult to modify. A long-term perspective is absolutely essential in change efforts, and then the efforts may be only partially successful or completely unsuccessful, even if the individual for whom the learning is intended is cooperative and strives to attain the hoped-for behavioral change. To change an entire culture (i.e., all of the human beings and what they do in that culture) in these personality areas is difficult beyond belief. "It takes a village," as the old Chinese saying goes. The whole culture must be changed, and that takes a tremendous amount of time and extraordinary skill.

In the next chapter we will examine some of the incidents of history that brought about most of the dependent (rather than independent) behavioral characteristics of many blacks today. Our basic assumption is this: obedience fosters dependent behavior. Obedience was required of blacks in America for more than fifteen generations. Little attention was devoted—by parents or others—to fostering a sense of personal responsibility, which can lead to independent behavior.

We have no data on this next issue at all, but it is our considered judgment that probably 65 to 70 percent of blacks in America today are independent, and 30 to 35 percent are probably dependent, as we define that term. In other words, we estimate that a majority of blacks have developed ways of thinking and feeling and acting in recent decades that resulted in most of them being truly independent today. Our best estimate of the percentage of whites who have achieved true independence would suggest that 85 to 90 percent have probably achieved that same level of independent behavior. But note: these are crude estimates, at best, and the figures may be "way off" in one way or another.

We use these figures simply to describe a reality about which we are fairly confident: most persons—black and white—are reasonably independent in their thinking and feeling and acting, and this sense of independence leads to the kinds of realistic and mature behavior that enables those same people to develop a sense of personal responsibility for how they function in daily life and what they do; responsibility for their own actions. And personal responsibility is the central ingredient of meaningful life in a democratic culture. Obedience is necessary to survive in an authoritarian situation. Responsibility is necessary to survive in a democratic situation. Further, responsibility must be learned and it must be taught in democratic situations, in the same way that obedience must be learned and it must be taught in authoritarian situations. Neither obedience nor responsibility is transmitted genetically from one generation to another. Both must be acquired through learning, primarily from one's parents and from one's immediate culture. Responsibility was probably never taught to black Americans from 1619 until about the 1950s. Obedience was the only item on the instructional agenda before the 1950s. These points comprise the core argument of our hypothesis, described above.

With this hypothesis we presume three things: many blacks (although it is undoubtedly a minor segment of the total black population) are basically dependent rather than independent in their outlook and behavior. Dependent people respond primarily to the concept of obedience rather than responsibility. Obedience can be achieved with authoritarian ways in short periods of time. Democracy requires people to be responsible, but it takes a long time to learn the art and essence—and the importance—of personal responsibility: years and years.

In the next chapter we will try to describe in detail some of the events that transpired over a very long period of time that assured obedience and development of dependent behavior among black Americans. Following that, we will review some of the research from various fields that describe the development and acquisition of personal responsibility, as we understand that term. That is, Chapter 4 will describe and explain. Chapter 5 will project and predict what might come to be. Chapter 6 will suggest one approach to solving the problem, albeit a bit late in the scheme of things.

Chapter 4
Dependence and Obedience Demanded for Fifteen Generations

Dependence is learned behavior. People are not born dependent, but become that way over time. There may be genetic predispositions toward such behavior, but we begin with the assumption that people learn to be dependent rather than being born that way. People are dependent when they are born, of course, because they are, by definition, weak and immature and incapable of existence without assistance. From the moment of birth forward, however, the thrust of human development is in the direction of autonomy and independence. People always need other people, in the best sense of that phrase, but they need other people to extend and further their own development toward autonomy and independence by providing encouragement, information, material things (e.g., food), and assistance. They neither need nor want to be dominated or encouraged to be deferential, subservient, or servile. People can and will learn to accept dependence—even slavery—if the system of rewards and punishments is designed to foster such behavior, but that is never their preference or their goal.

The conditions of slavery in early America were extended over such a long period, and the change from slavery to freedom and citizenship so complicated and fraught with hardship and danger over another long period of time, that the acculturation of youth that occurred within the black community regularly and continuously denied individual black persons a chance to learn to be truly independent. Instead, they learned to be dependent human beings. And it was the unbelievably long period of time involved that forced black Americans to acquire and develop the skills of dependency that enabled them to survive. It was not their idea. It was not their intention. It was imposed on them by dominant whites, but taught to them by black parents and other family members, who wanted them to survive. And it was not easy to move from dependency to autonomy when the domination finally receded; it was difficult beyond belief.

The immediate culture—parents and elders in the black community—taught black children in thousands of ways that they were dependent on their masters or other whites. "Breaking free" from the bondage was such a difficult task, and the instructions for children to learn to be dependent (or suffer and perhaps die) were so effective, even today many blacks in America have still not achieved a state of complete freedom for themselves and their loved ones. The basic point undergirding this hypotheses is that the terribly long time involved "taught" blacks in those situations that "being dependent rather than independent" was the only way to "make it" in the dominant white culture, and generation after generation after generation of blacks learned that lesson well. What is recognized as dependent behavior on the part of many blacks in America today is a consequence of that extended and traumatic time period (almost 350 years) in which the black culture—in order to survive—taught its young people to behave in dependent rather than independent ways.

Blacks are the way they are because they have been taught to behave that way (i.e., taught to be dependent) by the actions of white Americans. The driving force behind teaching blacks to be dependent started with the reality of slavery, but was perpetuated with the realities of prejudice, rejection, and humiliation. Blacks "learned to be dependent" because of the experiences imposed on them by whites through the institution of slavery, and through the experience of social rejection by whites after slavery officially ended with the "Emancipation Proclamation" and the Thirteenth Amendment.

Many forces and factors in society work in various ways to teach some individuals to develop "dependent behaviors;" it is not an "all or none" perspective at all. Blacks, however, have been subjected to humiliation and degradation far longer than whites, thus the proportion who experienced the acculturation that lead to dependency is understandable.

No other groups with which Americans are familiar or have even heard about have had such an extended period of slavery, rejection, and discrimination as blacks in the United States have experienced. Moses led the Jews out of bondage in Egypt, but that was thousands of years ago, and there is no evidence that the Jews were enslaved for centuries, nor were their families constantly broken apart. Jews imprisoned by the Germans in concentration camps in the 1940s were enslaved for only a few years, if they lived that long, as were the Russians that Stalin sent to the Gulag: less than a generation, at most. Individuals can cope with bondage, even for years, if they can survive, and if there is any kind of hope that they may be able to escape the situation at some point in the future. The complete loss of hope, which accompanies knowledge of the fact that the bondage might never end, is what produced dependent behavior in young black Americans for decades and decades and decades.

Black Americans were enslaved for more than ten generations initially—from the early 1600s to 1863, when they were emancipated by President Lincoln's proclamation—then they had to experience what came to be called "reconstruction" from about 1865 to 1876, which was divided sharply into two periods with different emphases: presidential reconstruction, with a negative emphasis; and congressional reconstruction, with a positive emphasis.

Beginning in the late 1870s, blacks in America were then subjected to what we will call "deconstruction" or "judicial tyranny" until 1948, when President Harry Truman integrated the armed forces of the United States by Presidential Order. Then in 1954, the Supreme Court made the decision to desegregate the schools. In 1964, the Civil Rights Act (patterned after a proposal that a Truman-appointed commission had developed in the 1940s, but which Congress had refused to enact into law) was finally passed at President Lyndon Johnson's prodding following President Kennedy's assassination. Since then, blacks have experienced the "growing pains" of more complete freedom, but those pains have been tainted to the present day with heavy doses of rejection and discrimination.

Our assumption is that, over time, black Americans perceived the "incidents" of the time (which later became historical "incidents") that affected their own psychological development: their sense of self, their sense of personal responsibility, and their sense of hope.

Many factors go together to make up one's "sense of self" and "sense of responsibility" and "sense of hope:" age, experience, intelligence, personality, values, aspirations, and the like. Two factors are especially important: locus of attention, and assignment of responsibility. And when we talk about these two factors, we want to talk about them *from the individual's point of view,* not from an external observer's point of view.

For example, we presume that every person tends to have a locus of attention which is assigned by the individual either "internal to self" or "external to self." That is, each of us tends to focus most of our attention upon who we are, what we are doing, what we want to do, and on and on. At other points in time we focus most of our attention on other people, on what we are reading, on the environment, on international affairs, but on what is happening external to self.

Further, we presume that every person tends to assign responsibility for what takes place in his or her own world either internal to self or external to self. Phrases such as "I can do it," "I am able to get that job done," "I am going to try to make such and so happen" all indicate that the individual has assigned responsibility internal to self. On the other hand, phrases such as "they made me do it," "it was not my idea, I am just doing what I was told to do," or "other people told me that this was a good idea, and I just went along" all indicate that the individual has assigned responsibility external to self: other people are in charge; it's not my fault.

In everyday life, these two aspects of self—locus of attention, and assignment of responsibility—tend to get juxtaposed in one of two primary ways. Either the individual develops an internal locus of attention and an external locus of control, or the individual develops an external locus of attention and an internal locus of control.

Those who have an internal locus of attention and an external locus of control are essentially self-absorbed: they think about themselves, they are concerned about themselves, they worry about how they look and how they dress and how they are perceived, but they think that other people have the power, other people have control, or fate or circumstances are in charge. Such persons tend to be followers rather than leaders, low achievers rather than high achievers, copiers rather than creative, and self-centered rather than other-centered.

Those who have an external locus of attention and an internal locus of control tend to be hard working, self-disciplined, organized, high achievers, creative and energetic people who are essentially other-centered rather than self-centered. These people seek out opportunities to assume responsibility. They exhibit a "can do" attitude: I can get the job done, we will figure out a way to make things happen, this is something we can handle.

The central idea of the dependence hypothesis stated earlier rests on the unbelievably long time period involved, and the comprehensiveness of the rejection and discrimination that accompanied and followed the period of enslavement. The accompanying experiences, through many decades, meant that young blacks—taught mostly by their parents—learned to be dependent in order to survive. The blacks who did not learn to be truly dependent were seen by whites as "too uppity," in the language of the day. That long acculturation process has made it difficult for many blacks, even today, to function as fully independent human beings: people who can make intelligent choices, people who have an external locus of attention and an internal locus of control, and people who understand and accept the consequences of unacceptable behavior, which is central to the concept of personal responsibility.

People who are dependent learn to be obedient. People who are independent learn to be responsible. One way to describe dependence is to think of it as an addiction—something without which one cannot get along—but it also implies lack of freedom. Freedom and slavery are opposites, of course, since slavery means bondage or a condition of submission to or dominance by someone or something, as illustrated above. In this sense, dependence is similar to "learned helplessness," as described by psychologists:

> Learned helplessness argues that organisms actively form a subjective representation of the degree to which an outcome is dependent upon responses. This representation has been variously called a perception, belief, or expectation of control. Of particular interest to helplessness theory is the situation in which responses and outcomes are noncontingently related. In this case, the theory claims that the organism forms the expectation that the outcome will be independent of its behavior and that this expectation causes motivational, cognitive, and emotional deficits. ***The hypothesized motivational deficit is a reduced incentive for initiating voluntary responses, and the cognitive deficit is a reduced ability to learn future response-reinforcer contingencies. The emotional consequence of learning that aversive outcomes are independent of responding is anxiety followed by depression.*** [5]

We realize that some blacks will be offended by what we have written here, but we do not mean to offend. We are trying to describe what we think happened in the past in order to understand and explain the realities today. We are convinced that the hypothesis set forth earlier in this chapter is testable, and we know that it can be supported by evidence or refuted. We think the hypothesis will stand the test. We think it will help explain "the race factor" in violent behavior, as we have described that idea here, and perhaps the hypothesis will generate insights that could be productive in helping young black citizens learn to be truly independent, in the best sense of that term.

Incidents That Affected Dependence Among Black Americans

We begin our discussion of historical factors that affected blacks and whites in America decades and decades ago with two statements which relate to the process of acculturation, although neither author would have called it that. Acculturation is generally a slow, gentle, unconscious process, but bit by bit, and over long periods of time, children's behavior is shaped by their elders in predetermined if not premeditated ways. Parents want their children to survive. They want their children "to make it" in the larger society. But survival is first and foremost in every parent's mind. "From Bombay to Missouri" was written by Mark Twain in 1895.

Incident: "From Bombay to Missouri," by Mark Twain

Our rooms were high up, on the front. A white man—he was a burly German—went up with us, and brought three natives along to see to arranging things. About fourteen others followed in procession, with the hand baggage; each carried an article—and only one; a bag, in some cases, in other cases less.

One strong native carried my overcoat, another a parasol, another a box of cigars, another a novel, and the last man in the procession had no load but a fan. It was all done with earnestness and sincerity, there was not a smile in the procession from the head of it to the tail of it. Each man waited patiently, tranquilly, in no sort of hurry, till one of us found time to give him a copper, then he bent his head reverently, touched his forehead with his fingers, and went his way. They seemed a soft and gentle race, and there was something both winning and touching about their demeanor.

There was a vast glazed door which opened upon the balcony. It needed closing, or cleaning, or something, and a native got down on his knees and went to work at it. He seemed to be doing it well enough, but perhaps he wasn't, for the burly German put on a look that betrayed dissatisfaction, then without explaining what was wrong, gave the native a brisk cuff on the jaw, and then told him where the defect was. It seemed such a shame to do that before us all. The native took it with meekness, saying nothing, and not showing in his face or manner any resentment. I had not seen the like of this for fifty years. It carried me back to my boyhood, and flashed upon me the forgotten fact that this was the usual way of explaining one's desires to a slave. I was able to remember that the method seemed right and natural to me in those days, I being born to it and unaware that elsewhere there were other methods; but I was also able to remember that those unresented cuffings made me sorry for the victim and ashamed for the punisher. My father was a refined and kindly gentleman, very grave, rather austere, of rigid probity, a sternly just and upright man, albeit he attended no church and never spoke of religious matters, and had no part nor lot in the pious jobs of his Presbyterian family, nor ever seemed to suffer from this deprivation. He laid his hand upon me in punishment only twice in his life, and then not heavily; once for telling him a lie—which surprised me, and showed me how unsuspicious he was, for that was not my maiden effort. He punished me those two times only, and never any other member of the family at all; yet every now and then he cuffed our harmless slave-boy, Lewis, for trifling little blunders and awkwardness. My father had passed his life among the slaves from his cradle up, and his cuffings proceeded from the custom of the time, not from his nature. When I was ten years old I saw a man fling a lump of iron ore at a slave-man in anger, for merely doing something awkwardly—as if that were a crime. It bounded from the man's skull, and the man fell and never spoke again. He was dead in an hour. I knew the man had a right to kill his slave if he wanted to, and yet it seemed a pitiful thing and somehow wrong, though why wrong I was not deep enough to explain if I had been asked to do it. Nobody in the village approved of that murder, but of course no one said much about it.

It is curious—the space annihilating power of thought. For just one second, all that goes to make me in me was in a Missourian village, on the other side of the globe, vividly seeing again those forgotten pictures of fifty years ago, and wholly unconscious of all things but those; and in the next second I was back in Bombay, and that kneeling native's smitten check was not done tingling yet. [6]

Incident: "A Reply to the Women of England," by Harriet Beecher Stowe

Along that same line, the following paragraphs were quoted by Harriet Beecher Stowe in "A Reply to the Address of the Women of England," published in *The Atlantic Monthly* magazine in January, 1863. The paragraphs are from a speech given on March 21, 1861, by Vice-President Alexander Stephens of the Confederate States of America. The speech describes a rationale for the South to secede from the Union. Quoting the speech by Stephens represented an effort by Ms. Stowe to persuade the women of England and Ireland to encourage their governments *not* to support the Confederacy during the war. Stowe's own argument, which occupied many pages in that January 1863 issue of *The Atlantic Monthly* magazine, was persuasive. In the section here, Stowe quotes a portion of Stephens' speech, which was given just a few days after Abraham Lincoln gave his First Inaugural Address.

*Last, not least, the new Constitution (of the Confederate States) has put to rest forever all the agitating questions relating to our peculiar institution,— African Slavery as it exists among us, the **proper status of the negro in our form of civilization. This was the immediate cause of the late rupture and present revolution . . . The prevailing ideas entertained by (Jefferson) and most of the leading statesmen at the time of the formation of the old Constitution were that the enslavement of the African was in violation of the laws of Nature, that it was wrong in principle, socially,***

morally, and politically. *It was an evil they knew not well how to deal with; but the general opinion of the men of that day was, that, somehow or other, in the order of Providence, the institution would evanescent, and pass away. The idea, though not incorporated in the Constitution, was the prevailing idea at the time. The Constitution, it is true, secured every essential guaranty to the institution, while it should last; and hence no argument can be justly used against the Constitutional guaranties thus secured, because of the common sentiment of the day.* ***Those ideas, however, were fundamentally wrong. They rested on the assumption of the equality of the races. This was an error.*** *It was a sandy foundation; and the idea of a government built upon it—when 'the storm came and the wind blew, it fell.'*

> ***Our new government is founded upon exactly the opposite ideas: its foundations are laid, its corner-stone rests, upon the great truth that the negro is not equal to the white man; that slavery, subordination to the superior race, is his natural and moral condition. (Applause.) This new government is the first in the history of the world, based upon this great physical, philosophical, and moral truth.*** [7]

Incident: Protests Against Slavery

Slavery was first introduced to the English colonies in America in 1619, and the earliest protest against slavery occurred in 1688. [8] In 1774, the Continental Congress voted non-intercourse with Great Britain, which included the following statement:

> *We will neither import nor purchase any slave imported after the first day of December next; after which time, we will wholly discontinue the slave trade, and will neither be concerned in it ourselves, nor will we hire our vessels, nor sell our commodities or manufactures to those who are concerned with this.* [9]

Incident: Massachusetts Court Decision, 1783

The status of slavery in Massachusetts was, throughout the Revolutionary period, a matter of uncertainty. In the case of *Quock Walker v. Nathaniel Jennison* in 1783, Jennison, who had been indicted for assault on Walker, justified his assault on the grounds that Walker was his slave. The Supreme Judicial Court, however, ruled that the first article of the Declaration of Rights had abolished slavery in Massachusetts. The case was not reported, but in 1874 Chief Justice Horace Gray read from the original notebook of Chief Justice Cushing, an extract from the 1783 decision that included the following statement:

> *Cushing, C. J. As to the doctrine of slavery and the right of Christians to hold Africans in perpetual servitude, and sell and treat them as we do our*

horses and cattle, that (it is true) has been heretofore countenanced by the Province Laws formerly, but nowhere is it expressly enacted or established. But whatever sentiments have formerly prevailed in this particular or slid in upon us by the example of others, a different idea has taken place with the people of America, more favorable to the natural rights of mankind, and to that natural, innate desire of Liberty, which with Heaven (without regard to color, complexion, or shape of noses-features) has inspired all the human race. And upon this ground our Constitution of Government, by which the people of this Commonwealth have solemnly bound themselves, sets out with declaring that all men are born free and equal—and that every subject is entitled to liberty, and to have it guarded by the laws, as well as life and property—and in short is totally repugnant to the idea of being born slaves. That being the case, I think the idea of slavery is inconsistent with our own conduct and Constitution; there can be no such thing as perpetual servitude of a rational creature, unless his liberty is forfeited by some criminal conduct or given up by personal consent or contract. [10]

Incident: The Northwest Ordinance, 1787

The Northwest Ordinance was adopted July 13, 1787, to provide "for the government of the Territory of the United States northwest of the River Ohio," and it included the following statement regarding slavery, written before the U.S. Constitution was adopted:

Art. 6. There shall be neither slavery nor involuntary servitude in the said territory, otherwise than in the punishment of crimes whereof the party shall have been duly convicted: Provided, always, That any person escaping into the same, from whom labor or service is lawfully claimed in any one of the original States, such fugitive may be lawfully reclaimed. [11]

Incident: Ratification of the United States Constitution, 1788

The Constitution of the United States was formally ratified by nine states by 1788 (the last of the thirteen states ratified it in 1790), and Congress by resolution fixed the date for the election of a President and the organization of the new government on September 13, 1788. The Constitution does not include the word "slave" anywhere, but Article I, Section 2 stipulates that "three fifths of all other Persons" shall be determined to apportion representation among the several States included within the Union. Section 9 of that same article says that the "Migration or Importation of such Persons as any of the States now existing shall think proper to admit, shall not be prohibited by the Congress prior to the Year one thousand eight hundred and eight." [12]

Incident: Decision by Supreme Court to Allow Citizens to Sue a State

In 1793, the Supreme Court of the United States made a decision in *Chisholm v. Georgia* that an individual citizen had a right to sue a State. [13] This decision was an affront to those who held that states were sovereign. Georgia, in fact, refused to appear before the Court, denied the validity of the judgment, and threatened to punish by death any official who attempted to execute the decree of the court. Other states also protested, and shortly after the decision an amendment was introduced which was ratified in 1798, and became the eleventh amendment to the Constitution.

> *Eleventh Amendment jurisprudence has become over the years esoteric and abstruse and the decisions internally inconsistent one with another and sometimes within the same decision. At the same time, it is a vital element of federal jurisdiction that "go[es] to the very heart of [the] federal system and affect[s] the allocation of power between the United States and the several states. Because of the centrality of the Amendment at the intersection of federal judicial power and the accountability of the States and their officers to federal constitutional standards, it has occasioned considerable dispute within the Court.* [14]

Incident: Prohibiting Further Importation of Slaves

In his sixth annual message, December 2, 1806, President Thomas Jefferson wrote:

> *I congratulate you, fellow citizens, on the approach of the period at which you may interpose your authority constitutionally to withdraw the citizens of the United States from all further participation in those violations of human rights which have been so long continued on the unoffending inhabitants of Africa.* [15]

Incident: Kentucky and Virginia Resolutions

In 1798, Kentucky and Virginia adopted resolutions that protested what was considered a dangerous usurpation of power by the federal government. The Kentucky Resolution was written by Thomas Jefferson, and the Virginia Resolution was written by James Madison. Both were based on the "states' rights" ideas, cornerstone arguments made primarily by Southern states in support of slavery and state sovereignty and in opposition to the supremacy of the Constitution of the United States. Every state from Maryland north replied to the Virginia and Kentucky Resolutions, disavowing the constitutional principles set forth in the resolutions. [16]

Incident: Missouri Compromise

The Missouri Compromise, finally agreed to after months of haggling in Congress, admitted Missouri as a slave state under certain conditions, which were agreed to by the state. The compromise was assumed to have settled the question regarding extension of slavery into the territories. [17]

Incident: Supreme Court Declares Law by Congress Unconstitutional

The first two cases in which the Supreme Court held a law of Congress void—*Marbury v. Madison* in 1803 and *Dred Scott v. Sandford* in 1857—both involved issues pertinent to slavery. The first case involved an issue in which the question arose: "Which holds precedence, the Constitution or a law passed by the Congress?" John Marshall answered the question by writing an opinion that the Constitution was uppermost. [18] The second case involved an issue in which the question arose: "Does a slave who is taken by his owner to a free state become free?" Roger Taney answered that question by writing the opinion that Scott (the slave) was not a citizen of the United States or of the State of Missouri, therefore was not competent to sue in Federal court. He remained a slave. Criticism of the process by which the decision was made by the Court erupted immediately after the decision and continues to the present era. [19]

Incident: South Carolina Nullification Controversy

In 1832, South Carolina passed an ordinance to nullify certain acts of the Congress of the United States. Andrew Jackson, a Southerner and states' right advocate, issued a proclamation to the people of South Carolina to uphold the Constitution of the United States. Jackson said:

> *The ordinance is founded, not on the indefeasible right of resisting acts which are plainly unconstitutional and too oppressive to be endured, but on the strange position that any one State may not only declare an act of Congress void, but prohibit its execution; that they may do this consistently with the Constitution; that the true construction of that instrument permits a State to retain its place in the Union and yet be bound by no other of its laws than those it may choose to consider as constitutional.*

> *. . . . If this doctrine had been established at an earlier day, the Union would have dissolved in its infancy. . . . I consider, then, the power to annul a law of the United States, assumed by one State, incompatible with the existence of the Union, contradicted expressly by the letter of the Constitution, unauthorized by its spirit, inconsistent with every principle on which it was*

founded, and destructive of the great object for which it was formed. . . . Because the Union was formed by a compact, it is said the parties to that compact may, when they feel themselves aggrieved, depart from it; but it is precisely because it is a compact that they can not. A compact is an agreement or binding obligation. It may by its terms have a sanction or penalty for its breach, or it may not. . . A government, on the contrary, always has a sanction, express or implied and expressly given. An attempt, by force of arms, to destroy a government is an offense, by whatever means the constitutional compact may have been formed; and such government has the right by the law of self defense to pass acts for punishing the offender, unless that right is modified, restrained, or resumed by the constitutional act. [20]

Incident: South Carolina Responds to President Andrew Jackson

South Carolina's responded to President Jackson's proclamation by resolving "that each state of the Union had the right, whenever it may deem such a course necessary for the preservation of its liberties or vital interests, to secede peaceably from the Union, and that there is no constitutional power in the general government, much less in the executive department, of that government, to retain by force such state in the Union." South Carolina then proceeded to adopt an ordinance "to nullify an act of Congress of the United States" on March 18, 1833.

We, the People of the State of South Carolina in Convention assembled, do Declare and Ordain, that the Act of the Congress of the United States, entitled "An Act further to provide for the collection of duties on imports," approved the second day of march, 1833, is unauthorized by the Constitution of the United States, subversive of that Constitution, and destructive of public liberty; and that the same is, and shall be deemed, null and void, within the limits of this state; and it shall be the duty of the Legislature, at such time as they may deem expedient, to adopt such measures and pass such acts as may be necessary to prevent the enforcement thereof, and to inflict proper penalties on any person who shall do any act in execution or enforcement of the same with the limits of this State. [21]

Incident: Anti-Slavery Society Formed

That same year (i.e., 1833), The American Anti-Slavery Society was formed, which South Carolina responded to in 1835 by adopting resolutions on abolitionist propaganda that urged other states to "promptly and effectually suppress all those associations within their respective limits, purporting to abolition societies, and that they will make it highly penal to print, publish, and distribute newspapers, pamphlets, tracts and pictorial representations calculated and having an obvious tendency to excite the slaves of the southern states to insurrection and revolt." [22]

Incident: Compromise of 1850

The Compromise of 1850, orchestrated by Henry Clay, produced an Omnibus Bill which covered the organization of the Territories, and a bill to prohibit the slave trade in the District of Columbia. [23]

Incident: Court Trial for Teaching Slaves to Read

The slave codes of most Southern states forbade teaching slaves to read or write. These laws were generally ignored, but Mrs. Douglas in Virginia was found guilty and sentenced to one month in jail. Portions of the judgment are described below:

> Upon an indictment found against you for assembling with negroes to instruct them to read and write, and for associating with them in an unlawful assembly, you were found guilty, and a mere nominal fine imposed, on the last day of this court held in the month of November. . . There are persons, I believe, in our community, opposed to the policy of the law in question. They profess to believe that universal intellectual culture is necessary to religious instruction and education, and that such culture is suitable to a state of slavery; and there can be no misapprehension as to your opinions on this subject, judging from the indiscreet freedom with which you spoke of your regard for the colored race in general. Such opinions in the present state of our society I regard as manifestly mischievous. It is not true that our slaves cannot be taught religious and moral duty, without being able to read the Bible and use the pen. [24]

Incident: Abraham Lincoln Delivers "A House Divided" Speech in Illinois

On June 17, 1858, Abraham Lincoln delivered a speech at the close of the Republican State Convention in Springfield, Illinois, in which he said the following:

> If we could first know where we are, and whither we are tending, we could better judge what to do, and how to do it. We are now far into the fifth year since a policy was initiated with the avowed object and confident promise of putting an end to slavery agitation. Under the operation of that policy, that agitation has not only not ceased, but has constantly augmented. In my opinion, it will not cease until a crisis shall have been reached and passed. "A house divided against itself cannot stand." I believe this government cannot endure permanently half slave and half free. I do not expect the Union to be dissolved; I do not expect the house to fall; but I do expect it will cease to be

divided. It will become all one thing, or all the other. Either the opponents of slavery will arrest the further spread of it, and place it where the public mind shall rest in the belief that it is in the course of ultimate extinction, or its advocates will push it forward till it shall become alike lawful in all the States, old as well as new, North as well as South. [25]

Incident: Wisconsin Supreme Court Refuses to Enforce Fugitive Slave Law

In 1859, two writs of custody to the supreme court of Wisconsin, Booth was held by Ableman, United States marshal, for violation of the fugitive slave law. The supreme court of Wisconsin discharged him from custody on a writ of *habeas corpus*. He was subsequently tried again before the United States district court, sentenced to imprisonment and fine. The supreme court of Wisconsin again ordered his release on the ground that the fugitive slave law was unconstitutional. [26]

Incident: John Brown's Last Speech

On November 2, 1859, John Brown, fanatical abolitionist, was tried for treason and sentenced to be hanged. Portions of his last speech are described below:

> *I have, may it please the Court, a few words to say. In the first place, I deny everything but what I have all along admitted—the design on my part to free the slaves. I intended certainly to have made a clean thing of that matter, as I did last winter, when I went into Missouri and there took slaves without the snapping of a gun on either side, moved them through the country, and finally left them in Canada. I designed to have done the same thing again, on a larger scale. That was all I intended. I never did intend murder, or treason, or the destruction of property, or to excite or incite slaves to rebellion, or to make insurrection.* [27]

Incident: Resolution Regarding Secession from Floyd County, Georgia, 1860

> *Whereas, the abolition sentiment of the Northern States first openly manifested in 1820, has for the last forty years, steadily and rapidly increased in volume, and in the intensity of hostility to the form of society, existing in the Southern States, and to the rights of these states as equal, independent and sovereign members of the Union; has led to long continued and ever increasing abuse and hatred of the Southern people; to ceaseless war upon their plainest Constitutional rights; to an open and shameless nullification of that provision of the constitution intended to secure the rendition of fugitive slaves, and of the laws of congress to give it effect; . . . has prompted the armed invasion of Southern soil, by stealth . . . for the diabolical purpose of*

inaugurating a ruthless war of the blacks against the whites throughout the Southern states; has prompted large masses of Northern people openly to sympathize with the treacherous and traitorous invaders of our country, and elevate the leader of a band of midnight assassins, and robbers . . to the rank of a hero and a martyr . . . .Therefore we, a portion of the people of Floyd County . . . do hereby declare: 1st. that Georgia is and of right ought to be a free, sovereign and independent state. 2nd. That she came into the Union with the other states, as a sovereignty, and by virtue of that sovereignty, has a right to secede whenever in her sovereign capacity she shall judge such a step necessary. [28]

Incident: Mississippi Resolutions on Secession, 1860

The Mississippi resolutions on secession were adopted on November 30, 1860, several months before Lincoln was inaugurated. Portions of those resolutions are reproduced below:

Whereas, The Constitutional Union was formed by the several states in their separate capacity for the purpose of mutual advantage and protection. . . . That the institution of slavery existed prior to the formation of the Federal Constitution, and is recognized by its letter, and all efforts to impair its value or lessen its duration by Congress, or any of the free States, is a violation of the compact of Union and is destructive of the ends for which it was ordained, but in defiance of the principles of the Union thus established, the people of the Northern states have assumed a revolutionary position toward the Southern states. [29]

Incident: Confederate States Adopt a Constitution

The Constitution of the Confederate States of America was adopted on March 11, 1861, one week after Abraham Lincoln was inaugurated as President of the United States. A provisional constitution had been adopted February 8, 1861, and in that document the African slave trade was prohibited. Described below is a brief section from the constitution that was adopted on March 11, 1861:

Sec. 2. (1) The citizens of each State shall be entitled to all the privileges and immunities of citizens of the several States, and shall have the right of transit and sojourn in any state of this Confederacy, with their slaves and other property; and the right of property in said slaves shall not be thereby impaired. . . . (3) No slave or other person held to service or labor in any State or territory of the Confederate States, under the laws thereof, escaping or unlawfully carried into another, shall, in consequence of any law or regulation therein, be discharged from such service or labor; but shall be delivered up on claim of the party to whom such slave belongs, or to whom such service or labor may be due. [30]

Incident: The Emancipation Proclamation

On January 1, 1863, Lincoln issued The Emancipation Proclamation, which had a major impact on both blacks and whites throughout the South, and even on the people of England. To blacks it was encouraging. The following is a short excerpt from the proclamation:

> *That on the 1st day of January, A.D. 1863, all persons held as slaves within any State or designated part of a State the people whereof shall be in rebellion against the United States shall be then, thenceforward, and forever free. [31]*

Incident: Lincoln's Plan for Reconstruction

In December 1863, before the presidential election scheduled to be held in 1864, Lincoln announced his plan of reconstruction. The plan provided for restoration of loyal governments in the seceded states. The presidential plan assumed that the states were not out of the Union, and that reconstruction was a presidential function, to be carried out through the pardoning power of the president. Many in Congress were opposed to this approach, and the Wade-Davis bill, based on different assumptions, was passed on July 8, 1864, but Lincoln did not sign the bill. [32] After Congress adjourned, Lincoln listed his reasons for refusing to sign the bill. Lincoln's approach was more forgiving. The Congressional approach was less forgiving.

Incident: General Sherman's Special Field Order No. 15

General William Tecumseh Sherman captured Atlanta in September 1864, then in November began what came to be called "Sherman's March to the Sea" toward Savannah, which was captured just before Christmas, 1864. After conferring with 20 black leaders, mostly Baptist and Methodist ministers, Sherman issued Special Field Order No. 15, which set aside the Sea Islands and some of the low country south of Charleston for black settlement. This incident was later referred to as the basis for the "forty acres and a mule" phrase, since each black family was assigned 40 acres of land, and many received an army mule. Blacks assumed that the land was to belong to them permanently, although Sherman later claimed it was a temporary measure, but more than forty thousand persons took up residence on the land by early summer, 1865. [33]

Incident: Admiral D. D. Porter's Perception of Lincoln's Terms for Peace, March 27, 1865

My opinion is, that Mr. Lincoln came down to City Point with the most liberal views toward the rebels. He felt confident that we would be successful, and was willing that the enemy should capitulate on the most favorable terms.

I don't know what the President would have done had he been left to himself, and had our army been unsuccessful, but he was then wrought up to a high state of excitement. He wanted peace on almost any terms, and there is no knowing what proposals he might have been willing to listen to. His heart was tenderness throughout, and, as long as the rebels laid down their arms, he did not care how it was done. I do not know how far he was influenced by General Grant, but I presume, from their long conferences, that they must have understood each other perfectly, and that the terms given to Lee after his surrender were authorized by Mr. Lincoln. I know that the latter was delighted when he heard that they had been given, and exclaimed, a dozen times, "Good!" "All Right!" "Exactly the thing!" and other similar expressions. Indeed, the President more than once told me what he supposed the terms would be: if Lee and Johnson surrendered, he considered the war ended, and that all the other rebel forces would lay down their arms at once. [34]

. . . Sherman asked the president, "What is to be done with the rebel armies when defeated? Lincoln replied at length, emphasizing his desire for reconciliation. He wanted to offer the most generous terms, he said, in order to "get the men comprising the Confederate armies back to their homes, at work on their farms and in their shops. . . they won't take up arms again. Let them go, officers and all. I want submission and no more bloodshed. . . . I want no one punished; treat them liberally all round. We want those people to return to their allegiance to the Union and submit to the laws. [35]

Incident: General Lee's Surrender at Appomattox Court House, April 9, 1865

Headquarters, Army of Northern Virginia
April 9, 1865

General: I have received your letter of this date containing the terms of the surrender of the Army of Northern Virginia, as proposed by you. As they are substantially the same as those expressed in your letter of the 8th instant, they are accepted. I will proceed to designate the proper officers to carry the stipulations into effect. [36]

R. E. Lee, General
[to] Lieutenant-General U. S. Grant

Incident: Confederate Soldiers Could Take Their Horses Home

During the meeting between Generals Grant and Lee regarding surrender terms, Lee explained that the horses of his cavalry and artillery were the property of his soldiers, and asked if these men could be permitted to keep their animals. Grant replied that the terms of the surrender would not allow this, but added:

> *I believe the war is now over, and that the surrender of this army will be followed soon by that of all the others; I know that the men, and indeed the whole South, are impoverished. I will not change the terms of the surrender, General Lee, but I will instruct my officers who receive the paroles to allow the cavalry and artillery men to retain their horses and take them home to work their little farms.* [37]

Grant declined to visit Richmond on his way back to Washington, arguing that his presence "might highlight demonstrations which would only wound the feelings of the residents, and we ought not to do anything at such a time which would add to their sorrow." [38]

Incident: Assassination of President Abraham Lincoln

After visiting Washington, D.C. and meeting with the president and his cabinet, Grant left the city for Philadelphia. He and his wife arrived at Broad Street station about midnight and went directly to Bloodgood's Hotel, where a telegraph messenger was waiting. A dispatch from the War Department was handed to Grant: "THE PRESIDENT WAS ASSASSINATED. RETURN TO WASHINGTON IMMEDIATELY." [39]

Incident: Adoption of the Thirteenth Amendment to the Constitution

In 1863 President Lincoln had issued the Emancipation Proclamation. There was doubt about the President's power to issue such an order at all, and a general conviction that its effect would not last beyond the restoration of the seceded States to the Union. The Thirteenth Amendment was proposed to solve this problem, and it was ratified in December 1865.

Section 1. Neither slavery nor involuntary servitude, except as punishment for crime whereof the party shall have been duly convicted, shall exist within the United States, or any place subject to their jurisdiction. [40]

Certain early cases suggested broad congressional powers, but the Civil Rights Cases of 1883 began a process, culminating in Hodges v. United States, which substantially curtailed these powers. In the former decision, the Court held unconstitutional an 1875 law guaranteeing equality of access to public accommodations. But the Court could not see that the refusal to any person of an accommodation at an inn or a place of public amusement, without any sanction or support from any state law, could inflict upon such person any manner of servitude or form of slavery. "It would be running the slavery argument into the ground to make it apply to every act of discrimination which a person may see fit to make." [41]

In 1968 (i.e., almost one hundred years later), the Supreme Court said as follows:

Surely Congress has the power under the Thirteenth Amendment rationally to determine what are the badges and the incidents of slavery, and the authority to translate that determination into effective legislation. . . Just as the Black Codes, enacted after the Civil War to restrict the free exercise of those rights, were substitutes for the slave system, so the exclusion of Negroes from white communities became a substitute for the Black Codes. And when racial discrimination herds men into ghettos and makes their ability to buy property turn on the color of their skin, then it too is a relic of slavery. [42]

Incident: President Andrew Johnson Issues Amnesty Proclamation

President Johnson issued an amnesty proclamation with the intention of restoring civil rights to most Southerners, although there were exceptions to the order: general officers in the Confederate army, West Point graduates who had resigned their commissions to serve with the Confederacy, and others. Individuals excluded from amnesty were encouraged to petition the President for a pardon. It was Grant's hope that Lee would petition President Johnson for a pardon. Many of the country's newspapers, however, pushed hard to try Lee and other generals for treason. [43]

Incident: Confrontation Between President Johnson and General Grant

In June 1865, Lee wrote Grant directly and enclosed his petition for clemency. Grant forwarded Lee's request to Secretary of War Stanton with a strong endorsement. Grant stipulated to Stanton that he did not think officers and men paroled at Appomattox could be tried for treason if they observed the terms of their parole. Grant also reminded Stanton that the terms of surrender at Appomattox had met with the approval of then-President Lincoln.

> *When Grant went to the White House, he found Johnson unyielding. The president said he wanted "to make treason odious," stating that Lee and other rebel leaders had to face punishment. Grant objected. . . .*
>
> *"When can these men be tried?" asked Johnson.*
>
> *"Never," replied Grant. "Never, unless they violate their parole. . . . I have made certain terms with Lee, the best and only terms. If I had told him and his army that their liberty would be invaded, that they would be open to arrest, trial, and execution for treason, Lee would have never surrendered, and we should have lost many lives in destroying him. My terms of surrender were according to military law, and so long as General Lee observes his parole, I will never consent to his arrest. I will resign the command of the army rather than execute any order to arrest Lee or any of his commanders so long as they obey the law."* [44]

This episode captures the spirit of Grant's philosophy regarding Reconstruction. During the years ahead, Grant regularly and repeatedly took action to assist the freedmen, and he confronted those at the state level who tried to make life miserable for blacks.

Incident: Establishment of the Freedmen's Bureau, 1865

> *Be it enacted, That there is hereby established in the War Department, to continue during the present war of rebellion, and for one year thereafter, a bureau of refugees, freedmen, and abandoned lands, to which shall be committed, as hereinafter provided, the supervision and management of all abandoned lands, and the control of all subjects relating to refugees and freedmen from rebel states, or from any district of country within the territory embraced in the operations of the army, under such rules and regulations as may be prescribed by the head of the bureau and approved by the President. The said bureau shall be under the management and control of a commissioner to be appointed by the President, by and with the consent of the Senate.* [45]

Incident: Black Codes of Mississippi, 1865

The so-called Black Codes represented the Southern effort to solve the problem of the freedmen. The codes varied in harshness. Most of these black laws were suspended by the military governors of the reconstructed states, and the Civil Rights Act and the Fourteenth Amendment were designed to protect the negro in his civil and legal rights.

Sec. 6. . . . All contracts for labor made with freedmen, free negroes, and mulattoes for a longer period than one month shall be in writing, and in duplicate, attested and read to said freedmen, free negro, or mulatto by a beat, city or county officer, or two disinterested white persons of the county in which the labor is to be performed. . . .

Sec. 7. . . . Every civil officer shall, and every person may, arrest and carry back to his or her legal employer any freedman, free negro, or mulatto who shall have quit the service of his or her employer before the expiration of his or her term of service without good cause; and said officer and person carrying back every deserting employee aforesaid the sum of five dollars, and ten cents per mile from the place of arrest to the place of delivery; and the same shall be paid by the employer, and held as a set-off for so much against the wages of said deserting employee. [46]

Incident: The Civil Rights Act, 1866

The Civil Rights Act was designed to protect the freedmen from discriminating legislation such as the "Black Codes" described above. This act was vetoed by President Andrew Johnson, then passed over his veto on April 9, 1866. The act conferred citizenship upon the negroes, legislation deemed necessary by the Dred Scott decision of the Supreme Court. Doubt as to its constitutionality induced Congress to enact most of its provisions into the Fourteenth Amendment to the Constitution. The Civil Rights Act was vetoed by President Johnson because it conferred citizenship, which the president argued was a prerogative of the states.[47]

Incidents: Acts of Congress Vetoed by President Johnson

In March 1867, Congress passed The Second Reconstruction Act, which was promptly vetoed by President Johnson. The Radicals in Congress and President Johnson were now "at logger heads," as the saying goes. Andrew Johnson, who was from Tennessee, had great sympathies for the South. He was not supportive of efforts that would restore the plantation owners to power, but he favored "white man's rule." His philosophy was very different from President Lincoln's, and he confronted the Radical members of Congress on many issues. This confrontation created tension among those who wanted to help the negro and those who wanted to assure "states' rights." Johnson was impeached, but the Senate failed to find him guilty. [48]

Incident: Fourteenth Amendment Ratified on July 28, 1868

Doubt about the Civil Rights Act of 1866 led to the formulation of this amendment to the Constitution. It was rejected by most of the Southern states, but ratification was made a condition of restoration to the Union, and it was ratified in July 1868. The Amendment, for the first time, defined citizenship, and for the first time provided the protection of the Federal Government around rights that might be invaded by state governments. The first section of the Amendment has given rise to more adjudication than any other part of the Constitution.

> *Article XIV, Sec. 1. All persons born or naturalized in the United States, and subject to the jurisdiction thereof, are citizens of the United States and the States wherein they reside. No state shall make or enforce any law which shall abridge the privileges or immunities of citizens of the United States; nor shall any State deprive any person of life, liberty, or property, without due process of law; nor deny to any person within its jurisdiction the equal protection of the laws.* [49]

Incident: Veto of Freedmen's Bureau Bill, 1866

The Freedmen's Bureau had been established in act of Congress in 1865. In February 1866, a new Freedmen's Bureau bill, extending the life of the bureau and enlarging its powers, was presented to President Johnson, who vetoed it. The veto of the bill inaugurated open hostilities between the Congressional Radicals and President Johnson. [50]

Incidents: Reaction of Southerners to Negro Suffrage

> *Initially, Grant put his trust in the ballot box. He worked mightily to secure the adoption of the Fifteenth Amendment, believing the rights of freedmen would be protected once they enjoyed the franchise. Grant was not alone in that belief. When the amendment was adopted, abolitionist leader William Lloyd Garrison proclaimed that nothing equaled "this wonderful, quiet, sudden transformation of four million human beings from . . . the auction-block to the ballot box . . . But neither Grant, the reformers, or the Republicans in Congress foresaw the virulence of white Southern opposition to Negro suffrage, or the proclivity for violence in states where respect for law and order had eroded substantially. Led by the Ku Klux Klan, masked riders introduced a reign of terror in the South. Black schools were burned, teachers beaten, voters intimidated, and political opponents of both races kidnapped and murdered.* [51]

> *As the Klan grew bolder and the death toll mounted, Southern Republicans desperately petitioned Washington for help. Traditionally, crimes such as murder, arson, and assault fell within the jurisdiction of state and local authorities, yet most law enforcement officials in the South refused to move against the Klan.* [52]

In the North Carolina piedmont, where federal troops sent by Grant helped apprehend suspects, hundreds of men were indicted. In northern Mississippi, where Klan violence was endemic, tenacious United States attorneys secured nearly 1,000 indictments in the early 1870s, and fully 55 percent of the cases resulted in conviction. But in many localities Klan terrorism continued unabated, with violence peaking at election time. . . South Carolina observers listed 227 "outrages" in one county, 118 in another, and 300 in a third. In North Carolina, Klan terrorism helped the Democrats recapture the state, electing five of seven congressmen. "An organized conspiracy is in existence in every County of the State, and its aim is to control the government," Governor William H. Holden wrote Grant. [53]

Incident: Adoption of the Fifteenth Amendment to the Constitution, 1870

Section 1. The right of citizens of the United States to vote shall not be denied or abridged by the United States or by any State on account of race, color, or previous condition of servitude. [54]

Incident: Grant Pressures Congress to Pass Ku Klux Klan Bill

Congress convened on March 4, and . . . five days after the session began, [Grant] requested special legislation that would authorize the government to suppress the Klan . . . . By mid-March it was apparent the Ku Klux Klan bill was headed for defeat . . . . Confronted with what appeared to be certain defeat, Grant took the offensive . . . [and] with his entire cabinet in attendance, Grant made a rare visit to Capitol Hill . . . . Congress enacted the Ku Klux Klan bill on April 20, 1871. [55]

The efforts of Akerman and the Department of Justice paid quick dividends. Throughout the South the Klan was put on the defensive. Federal grand juries returned more than 3,000 indictments in 1871. The attorney general allowed those who confessed and identified the organization's leaders to escape without punishment, while bringing the worst offenders to jail. About 600 were convicted. . . By 1872 Grant's willingness to bring the full legal authority of the government to bear had broken the Klan's back and produced a dramatic decline in violence throughout the South. [56]

Incident: Supreme Court Invalidates the Enforcement Act of 1870

Grant had appointed four persons to the Supreme Court, but only one voted to sustain the government's effort to protect the freedmen.

*In **United States v. Reese**, a voting rights case arising in Kentucky, the Court invalidated the operative sections of the Enforcement Act of 1870,* *holding that the Fifteenth Amendment did not confer the right of suffrage in state and local elections. The same day that **Reese** was handed down, the Court also gutted enforcement of the Ku Klux Klan Act. Speaking once more for his colleagues, this time in **United States v. Cruikshank**, Waite said the Fourteenth and Fifteenth amendments applied only to action by the states, not individuals. "The power of Congress to legislate [to enforce the amendments] does not extend to the passage of laws for the suppression of ordinary crimes within the States. That duty was originally assumed by the States, and it still remains there." [57]*

Incident: Fourteenth Amendment to the United States Constitution

Section 1. All persons born or naturalized in the United States, and subject to the jurisdiction thereof, are citizens of the United States and the State wherein they reside. No State shall make or enforce any law which shall abridge the privileges or immunities of citizens of the United States; nor shall any State deprive any person of life, liberty, or property, without due process of law; nor deny to any person within its jurisdiction the equal protection of the laws. [58]

*In the **Dred Scott Case**, Chief Justice Taney for the Court ruled that United States citizenship was enjoyed by two classes of individuals: (1) white persons born in the United States as descendants of "persons, who were at the time of the adoption of the constitution recognized as citizens in the several States and [who] became also citizens of this new political body," the United States of America, and (2) those who, having been "born outside the dominions of the United States," had migrated thereto and been naturalized therein. The States were competent, he continued, to confer state citizenship upon anyone in their midst, but they could not make the recipient of such states a citizen of the United States. The Negro, according to the Chief Justice, was ineligible to attain United States Citizenship, either from a State or by virtue of birth in the United States, even as a free man descended from a Negro residing as a free man in one of the States at the date of ratification of the Constitution. Congress, first in Art. 1 of the Civil Rights Act of 1866, and then in the first sentence of Art. 1 of the Fourteenth Amendment, set aside the Dred Scott holding in a sentence "declaratory of existing rights, and affirmative of existing law." [59]*

Incident: Slaughter-House Cases Nullify Effects of Fourteenth Amendment

Unique among constitutional provisions, the privileges and immunities clause of the Fourteenth Amendment enjoys the distinction of having rendered a "practical nullity" by a single decision of the Supreme Court issued within five years after its ratification. In the Slaughter-House Cases, a bare majority of the Court frustrated the aims of the most aggressive sponsors of this clause, to whom was attributed an intention to centralize "in the hands of the Federal Government large powers hitherto exercised by the States" with a view to enabling business to develop unimpeded by state interference. . . To have fostered such intentions, the Court declared, would have been "to transfer the security and protection of all the civil rights . . . to the Federal Government, . . . to bring within the power of Congress the entire domain of civil rights heretofore belonging exclusively to the States," and to "constitute this court a perpetual censor upon all legislation of the States, on the civil rights of their own citizens, with authority to nullify such as it did not approve as consistent with those rights, as they existed at the time of the adoption of this amendment. [60]

Incidents: Perversion of Original Purpose of the Fourteenth Amendment

Our interpretation of most of the decisions by the Supreme Court of the United States relative to the Fourteenth Amendment to the Constitution suggests that the basic purpose of the Amendment was perverted. Our dictionary (i.e., *Webster's II New College Dictionary*) defines "pervert" as "1. to cause to turn from what is considered morally right : corrupt. . . 3. to use incorrectly : misuse. . . 4. to interpret incorrectly : misconstrue."

We are not constitutional lawyers, but it is difficult to follow the logic of the Court in reasoning that "no State shall make or enforce any law which shall abridge the privileges or immunities of citizens of the United States" to questions that dealt almost exclusively with such concerns as hours of work, labor in mines, employment of children, minimum wage laws, workmen's compensation laws, collective bargaining, grade crossings, regulations of business, laws prohibiting trusts, laws regulating boards of trade, pharmacies, regulation of corporations, laws prohibiting restraint of trade, purchase of harvesting or threshing machinery, oil and gas, fish and game, location of dairy stables, sewers, garbage, water supply, making railroads liable for damage caused by operation of their locomotives, use of public lands for grazing, sale of intoxicating liquors, abandoned property, exempting sellers of ready to wear glasses replace lenses without prescriptions, administration of estates, cremation of garbage, red light districts in a city, protection of dogs, solid waste disposal, advertising, keeping billiard halls for hire, bread sold in loaves must be standardized in size, regulation of fire insurance rates, sprinkler systems in buildings of nonfireproof construction, exemption of buses from net load and length of trucks, destruction of cedar trees to protect apple orchards, prohibiting sale of capital stock on margin, taxes on insurance companies, food stamp programs, Sunday blue laws, income taxes, franchise taxes, real property taxes, taxes on intangibles, corporate privilege taxes, eminent domain, suability of foreign corporations, entrapment, and the like. [61]

We cite these topics—all instances in which cases have been argued and decided on the basis of the Fourteenth Amendment, few of which relate to the purpose for which the amendment was originally proposed—as examples of what we think resulted in a kind of "judicial tyranny" or "judicial prejudice" against the notion of equality for blacks that existed from the end of the Civil War until the middle of the 20th century. *From the 1860s until the 1950s, the Supreme Court of the United States was loathe to deny states complete freedom to enact and enforce laws which discriminated against black Americans, despite the ratification of the Thirteenth, Fourteenth, and Fifteenth Amendments to the Constitution.*

> *In the case in which it was first called upon to interpret this clause (i.e., "persons"), the Court doubted whether "any action of a State not directed by way of discrimination against the [N]egroes as a class, or on account of their race, will ever be held to come within the purview of this provision." [62]*

The Supreme Court selects the cases on which it agrees to hear arguments. We did not have access to the list of cases submitted to the Court requesting a hearing by the Court, but it is hard to believe that none were proposed that involved discrimination against blacks. If few were presented, that proves our point: blacks were intimidated and forced into dependent roles.

Incident: *Plessy v. Ferguson* Decision by the Supreme Court

> *Cases decided soon after ratification of the Fourteenth Amendment may be read as precluding any state-imposed distinction based on race, but the Court in **Plessy v. Ferguson** adopted a principle first propounded in litigation attacking racial segregation in the schools of Boston, Massachusetts. **Plessy** concerned not schools but a state law requiring the furnishing of "equal but separate" facilities for rail transportation and requiring the separation of white and Negro passengers. "The object of the [Fourteenth] {A}mendment was undoubtedly to enforce the absolute equality of the two races before the law, but in the nature of things it could not have been intended to abolish distinctions based upon color, or to enforce social, as distinguished from a political, equality, or a commingling of the two races upon terms unsatisfactory to either. Laws permitting, or even requiring their separation in places where they are liable to be brought into contact do not necessarily imply the inferiority of either race to the other, and have been generally, if not universally, recognized as within the competency of the state legislatures in exercise of their police power. The Court observed that a common instance of this type of law was the separation of race of children in school, which had been upheld, it was noted, "even by courts of states where the political rights of the colored race have been longest and most earnestly enforced."*

> *Subsequent cases following **Plessy** that actually concerned school segregation did not expressly question the doctrine and the Court's decision*

*assumed its validity. It held, for example, that a Chinese student was not denied equal protection by being classified with Negroes and sent to school with them rather than with whites (**Gong Lum v. Rice**, 275 U.S. 78, 1927), and it upheld the refusal of an injunction to require a school board to close a white high school until it opened a high school for Negroes (**Cummings v. Board of Education,** 175 U.S. 528, 1899). [63]*

Incident: John M. Harlan's Dissent in Plessy v. Ferguson

The Plessy case grew out of a Louisiana law passed in 1890 that required railroads to provide "separate but equal" accommodations for white and colored passengers. On June 2, 1892, Homer Plessy, who was only one-eighth Negro and appeared to be white, boarded a train in New Orleans and took a vacant seat in a coach reserved for white persons. The conductor ordered Plessy to move to a coach for colored passengers, but he refused. With the aid of a police officer Plessy was thereupon forcibly ejected from the train, locked up in the New Orleans jail, and taken before a judge Ferguson to answer a charge of violating the Louisiana law. In affirming his conviction, the Supreme Court of Louisiana upheld the state statue. Plessy then appealed to the Supreme Court.

Two southerners—[John] Harlan and Justice Edward D. White of Louisiana—sat on the Court when the Plessy case was decided. . . The majority opinion, written by Justice Henry B. Brown, Michigan's first Supreme Court justice, was supported by all the participating justices except Harlan. Plessy's lawyers had argued that the Louisiana segregation law was unconstitutional under both the Thirteenth Amendment of the Constitution, abolishing slavery, and the equal protection clause of the Fourteenth Amendment. . . Plessy's argument that segregation branded the Negro with a badge of inferiority was curtly dismissed by Justice Brown with the incredible assertion that "if this is so, it is not by reason of anything found in the act, but solely because the colored race chooses to put that construction on it."

*Harlan's solitary dissenting opinion has been justly characterized as one of the most vigorous and forthright dissents in Supreme Court history. . . Segregation, to Harlan, **was** discrimination against the Negro. He remarked, everyone knows that the statute in question had its origin in the purpose, not so much to exclude white persons from railroad cars occupied by blacks, as to exclude colored people from coaches occupied by or assigned to white persons. Railroad corporations of Louisiana did not make discrimination among whites in the matter of accommodation for travelers. The thing to accomplish was, under the guise of giving equal accommodations for whites and blacks, to compel the latter to keep to themselves while traveling in* *railroad passenger coaches. No one would be so wanting in candor as to assert the contrary. The fundamental objection, therefore, to the statute is that it interferes with the personal freedom of citizens. . . . If a white man and a black man choose to occupy the same public conveyance on a public highway, it is their right to do so, and no government, proceeding alone on grounds of race, can prevent it without infringing the personal liberty of each. . . .*

Our Constitution is color-blind, and neither knows nor tolerates classes among citizens. In respect of civil rights all citizens are equal before the law. The humblest is the peer of the most powerful. The law regards man as man, and takes no account of his surroundings or of his color when his civil rights as guaranteed by the supreme law of the land are involved. It is, therefore, to be regretted that this high tribunal, the final expositor of the fundamental law of the land, has reached the conclusion that it is competent for a State to regulate the enjoyment of citizens of their civil rights solely upon the basis of race. . . . The arbitrary separation of citizens, on the basis of race . . . is a badge of servitude wholly inconsistent with the civil freedom and the equality before the law established by the Constitution. It cannot be justified upon any legal ground. [64]

Our basic point is that people who are dependent must learn to be obedient. People who are independent must learn to be responsible. For almost 300 years, the acculturation of blacks (carried out by black parents, but imposed on blacks by the dominant white culture) fostered the development of dependent rather than independent behaviors.

An Experimental Approach to Obedience

We think that our hypothesis, stated earlier in this chapter, may help explain why the murder rate of black males (primarily by other black males) is extremely high. We restate our hypothesis here, and offer it as a partial explanation, at least, of introducing "the race factor" into the discussion of "murder in America," as presented in these pages. The hypothesis follows:

Blacks in early America grew up in a culture of slavery and were acculturated over an extremely long period of time to be dependent (rather than independent) human beings. After emancipation and amendments to the Constitution assuring equality, the intransigence of whites and the refusal of courts to legitimize equality fostered the development of "learned helplessness" on the part of many blacks. Incremental steps by the federal government in the direction of equality in mid-twentieth century eventually led to frustration and then aggression rather than reason and persuasion to resolve disagreements. Independent and responsible behavior began to

develop throughout the black community toward the end of the twentieth century, following changes in both policies and structures of the federal government, but black males, especially, continue to engage in aberrant behaviors.

Obedience is based on fear. Responsibility is based on understanding. Persons who are dependent must learn to be obedient. Persons who are independent must learn to be responsible. The dominant white culture in the South focused on teaching blacks to be obedient (and thus dependent) rather than responsible (and thus independent), for hundreds of years.

In the 1950s, a psychologist set out to study obedience in experimental ways. He wrote:

Obedience is as basic an element in the structure of social life as one can point to. Some system of authority is a requirement of all communal living, and it is only the person dwelling in isolation who is not forced to respond, with defiance or submission, to the commands of others. For many people, obedience is a deeply ingrained behavior tendency, indeed a potent impulse overriding training in ethics, sympathy, and moral conduct.

The dilemma inherent in submission to authority is ancient, as old as the story of Abraham, and the question of whether one should obey when commands conflict with conscience has been argued by Plato, dramatized in Antigone, and treated to philosophical analysis in almost every historical epoch. Conservative philosophers argue that the very fabric of society is threatened by disobedience, while humanists stress the primacy of the individual conscience. [65]

Stanley Milgram went on to describe a series of experiments in social psychology that he conceptualized in the 1950s and 1960s to determine how most people behave in concrete situations. Stories about how the Germans had treated Jews under Hitler's regime had surfaced during the Second World War, but it was only at the end of the war and in the years immediately following that the full story came to light, and people all over the world were dumbfounded at both the extent and the details of the persecution. Those stories led Milgram to conduct research studies that would not be permissible today, but which led to deeper understandings of obedience than had existed before.

In the basic experimental designs two people come to a psychology laboratory to take part in a study of memory and learning. One of them is designated a "teacher" and the other a "learner." The experimenter explains that the study is concerned with the effects of punishment on learning. The learner is conducted into a room, seated in a kind of miniature electric chair, his arms are strapped to prevent excessive movement, and an electrode is attached to his wrist. He is told that he will be read lists of simple word pairs, and that he will then be tested on his ability to remember the second word of a pair when he hears the first one again. Whenever he makes an error, he will receive electric shocks of increasing intensity.

The real focus of the experiment is the teacher. After watching the learner being strapped into place, he is seated before an impressive shock generator. The instrument panel consists of thirty level switches set in a horizontal line. Each switch is clearly labeled with a voltage designation ranging from 14 to 450 volts. The following designations are clearly indicated for groups of four switches, going from left to right: Slight Shock, Moderate Shock, Strong Shock, Very Strong Shock, Intense Shock, Extreme Intensity Shock, Danger: Severe Shock. (Two switches after this last designation are simply marked XXX.) When a switch is depressed, a pilot light corresponding to each switch is illuminated in bright red; an electric buzzing is heard; a blue light, labeled "voltage energizer," flashes; the dial on the voltage meter swings to the right; and various relay clicks sound off.

The upper left hand corner of the generator is labeled SHOCK GENERATOR, TYPE ZLB. DYSON INSTRUMENT COMPANY, WALTHAM, MASS., OUTPUT 15 VOLTS — 450 VOLTS.

Each subject is given a sample 45 volt from the generator before his run as a teacher, and the jolt strengthens his belief in the authenticity of the machine.

The teacher is a genuinely naïve subject who has come to the laboratory for the experiment. The learner, or victim, is actually an actor who receives no shock at all. The point of the experiment is to see how far a person will proceed in a concrete and measurable situation in which he is ordered to inflict increasing pain on a protesting victim.

Conflict arises when the man receiving the shock begins to show that he is experiencing discomfort. At 75 volts, he grunts; at 120 volts, he complains loudly; at 150, he demands to be released from the experiment. As the voltage increases, his protests become more vehement and emotional. At 285 volts, his response can be described only as an agonized scream. Soon thereafter, he makes no sound at all.

For the teacher, the situation quickly becomes one of gripping tension. It is not a game for him; conflict is intense and obvious. The manifest suffering of the learner presses him to quit: but each time he hesitates to administer a shock, the experimenter orders him to continue. To extricate himself from this plight, the subject must make a clear break with authority. . . .

Before the experiments, I sought predictions about the outcome from various kinds of people — psychiatrists, college sophomores, middle-class adults, graduate students, and faculty in the behavioral sciences. With remarkable similarity, they predicted that virtually all subjects would not go beyond 150 volts, when the victim makes his first explicit demand to be freed. They expected that only 4 percent would reach 300 volts, and that only a pathological fringe of about one in a thousand would administer the highest shock on the board.

These predictions were unequivocally wrong. Of the forty subjects in the first experiment, twenty-five obeyed the orders of the experimenter to the end, punishing the victim until they reached the most potent shock available on the generator. After 450 volts were administered three times, the experimenter called a halt to the session. Many obedient subjects then heaved sighs of relief, mopped their brows, rubbed their fingers over their eyes, or nervously fumbled cigarettes. Others displayed only minimal signs of tension from beginning to end.

When the very first experiments were carried out, Yale undergraduates were used as subjects, and about 60 percent of them were fully obedient. . . when the experiments were repeated in Princeton, Munich, Rome, South Africa, and Australia, the level of obedience was invariably somewhat higher than found in the investigation reported in this article. Thus one scientist in Munich found 85 percent of his subjects obedient. . . .

The subjects do not derive satisfaction from inflicting pain, but they often like the feeling they get from pleasing the experimenter. They are proud of doing a good job, obeying the experimenter under difficult circumstances. While the subjects administered only mild shocks on their own initiative, one experimental variation showed that, under orders, 30 percent of them were willing to deliver 450 volts even when they had to forcibly push the learner's hand down on the electrode. . . .

The essence of obedience is that the person comes to view himself as the instrument for carrying out another person's wishes, and he therefore no longer regards himself as responsible for his actions. Once this critical shift of viewpoint has occurred, all of the essential features of obedience follow.

The most far-reaching consequence is that the person feels responsible to the authority directing him, but feels no responsibility for the content of the actions that the authority prescribes. Morality does not disappear — it acquires a radically different focus: the subordinate person feels shame or pride depending on how adequately he has performed the actions called for by authority. [66]

These findings by Milgram are related, in some ways, to the observations that Daniel Goldhagen reported in his doctoral dissertation at Harvard, which was later published as a book, *Hitler's Willing Executioners.* [67] Goldhagen's work was recognized as an outstanding dissertation, even though some historians questioned his historiography, but it is major research piece on the subject. The book described ordinary Germans willingly executing Jews because they had been directed to by authorities.

This chapter examined the logic and research related to the first half of our hypothesis. Chapter 5 will examine the logic and research related to the second half of the hypothesis.

Chapter 5
Independence and Responsibility
Encouraged for Two Generations

Introduction

If Lincoln had not been assassinated in 1865, America might have become a different, better place for black Americans than it became after he was killed. But the assassination took place, and Lincoln died. Andrew Johnson succeeded Lincoln in the White House. America remained divided, and the nation's ability to cope with race problems regressed for decades after Lincoln's death, although many people worked tirelessly to help the reunited states resume the commitments to equality and freedom that blossomed briefly during Reconstruction, following the war-torn Lincoln years. Political leaders in southern states were adamant, though, and Southern thought and values dominated the American agenda for another hundred years. The Democratic political party prevailed in the South, as it had for the previous century, and the regression was secure.

World War II ended in 1945. Franklin Roosevelt died in April, 1945, and Harry Truman assumed the presidency during the final months of that horrific war. When America dropped the atom bomb in August of that year, Japan surrendered. American service men and women headed home. Thousands of black Americans had served their country throughout the conflict, though most had been relegated to service rather than combat roles because of the persisting racial discrimination that still characterized the United States at that time. Even after having proved themselves as "fit for battle" during the Civil War, almost a hundred years earlier, tradition and stereotyping denied most blacks opportunities to "prove their worth" in fighting units of the armed forces during the Second World War. They were "allowed" to serve their country as cooks and mechanics, but seldom as riflemen or airplane pilots. Subjugation and discrimination were still alive and well in America's military might.

In February, 1946, a black American from New York city, Sergeant Isaac Woodard, Jr., discharged after honorable military service, went into Batesburg, South Carolina, in military uniform, three hours after his discharge. Arriving in Batesburg, he was immediately set upon by a group of white men in that city, including the police chief, Lynwood Lanier Shull. Attacked physically and beaten savagely, his eyes were gouged out by the attackers, and he was rendered blind for the rest of his life. "Sheriff Shull acknowledged on the witness stand that the physical force he used on Sergeant Woodard resulted in one of Woodard's eyes being gouged out and in the other eye being so badly damaged that the young sergeant was blinded for life." [1]

President Harry Truman, born and raised in Missouri and whose mother was an ardent segregationist, had served as a captain in the United States Army during World War I, was outraged by the incident in South Carolina. He ordered federal authorities to pursue the possibility of criminal charges. Following the pretense of a trial, all of the alleged perpetrators were adjudged "not guilty" after 30 minutes of deliberation by a local, all white jury, and the crime against the black veteran went unpunished. [2]

Truman did not to get angry, but he was determined to get even: to do right. He set in motion efforts to persuade some of the most honorable and respected men and women in the nation to form a Civil Rights Commission, and he encouraged the commission to make recommendations to the President and Congress that, if adopted as law, would insure every citizen—black or white—of fair and equitable treatment as true citizens of the United States. Truman was determined to avenge by law the humiliation and hurt imposed by whites against blacks throughout America, but especially in the South. The violence against the returning black soldier in South Carolina triggered his resolve to right a massive wrong. The work of the Civil Rights Commission was to be a vehicle of change in an America dedicated to improving opportunities and expanding freedoms for all citizens. [3]

The "solid South," however, vowed otherwise. Democrats, as a political party, had dominated the South for more than a century. Following Thomas Jefferson's lead against Alexander Hamilton's push for a strong central government, Jefferson's push for "states' rights" had united the South against any effort to cope creatively or intelligently with the "peculiar institution" of slavery. Jefferson had encouraged Congress to restrict importing slaves into the country after 1808, as the Constitution had specified, but his ambivalence toward slavery had obscured his vision about how and when the scourge of slavery might be ameliorated.

Then the *Dred Scott v. Sandford* decision in 1856 and the *Plessey v. Ferguson* decision in 1896 seemingly "locked down" discussion of segregation and discrimination against blacks forever. In 1954, however, sixty years after the *Plessey* decision, the Supreme Court of the United States finally reversed its historical stance (what we characterize as "judicial tyranny" against blacks) and, in a unanimous decision, declared segregated schools unconstitutional.

*"Separate but equal" was formally abandoned in **Brown v. Board of Education**, involving challenges to segregation **per se** in the schools of four states in which the lower courts had found that the schools provided were equalized or were in the process of being equalized. Though the Court had asked for argument on the intent of the framers, extensive research had proved inconclusive, and the Court asserted that it could not "turn the clock back to 1867 . . . or even to 1896 . . ." but must consider the issue in the context of the vital importance of education in 1954. Denial of opportunity to an adequate education must often be a denial of the opportunity to succeed in life, separation of the races in the schools solely on the basis of race must necessarily generate feelings of inferiority in the disfavored race   adversely*

affecting education as well as other matters, and therefore the equal protection clause was violated by such separation. We conclude that in the field of public education the doctrine of "separate but equal" has no place. Separate educational facilities are inherently unequal. [4]

After hearing argument on the remedial order which should issue, the Court remanded the cases to the lower courts to adjust the effectuation of its mandate to the particularities of each school district. "At stake is the personal interest of the plaintiffs in admission to public schools as soon as practicable on a nondiscriminatory basis". . . but . . . the lower courts were to require compliance "with all deliberate speed." [5] In the early 1960's, various state practices—school closings, minority transfer plans, zoning, and the like—were ruled inadmissible and it was indicated that the time was running out for full implementation of the **Brown** *mandate.* [6]

About this time, "freedom of choice" plans were promulgated under which each child in the school district could choose each year which school he wished to attend and, subject to space limitations, he could attend that school. . . Enactment of Title VI of the Civil Rights Act of 1964 and HEW enforcement in a manner as to require effective implementation of affirmative actions to desegregate led to a change of attitude in the lower courts, and to a three-case decision in the Supreme Court posited on the principle that the only desegregation plan permissible is one which actually results in the abolition of the dual school, and charging school officials with an affirmative obligation to achieve it. School boards must present to the district courts "a plan that promises realistically to work and promises realistically to work now," in such a manner as "to convert promptly to a system without a 'white' school and a 'Negro' school, but just schools" . . . school desegregation encompassed not only the abolition of dual attendance systems for students but faculty, staff, and services merging as well into one system so that no school could be marked as either a "black" or a "white" school. [7]

The Civil Rights Act of 1964, pushed through Congress by President Lyndon Johnson following President Kennedy's assassination in 1963, was based essentially on President Truman's Civil Rights Commission's report of 1947. The *Brown* decision of 1954 and the Civil Rights Movement, under the leadership of Martin Luther King, Jr., which began about the same time, finally forced other members of Congress to override Southern Congressional members' concerns and prejudices and enact the Civil Rights Act of 1964. When he signed the bill, however, Johnson, who had always voted in favor of pro-segregation policies while a member of Congress, [8] supposedly said "there goes the South." [9]

Johnson's prescience was correct. Southern Democrats in Congress, who had always been conservative, moved, one by one, to switch their allegiance to the Republican party, and that transformation continues to this day. Those changes did not represent changes in philosophy among Southern politicians, only changes in political parties.

Democrats in the South were never "liberal," in the general meaning of that term; they were always "conservative." The Democratic Party was the political party that supported slavery and subjugation of blacks in the 1820s and throughout the Civil War, all the way to the 1920s. Lincoln's Whig Party and then the newly formed Republican Party were the anti-slavery parties in pre-Civil War years, and Grant as a Republican continued that emphasis when he served as president following the Civil War. The conservative philosophies of Harding, Coolidge, and Hoover, however, led to economic stagnation in the South in the first part of the twentieth century. Franklin D. Roosevelt forged a new political coalition in the 1930s that modified the general public's perception of the Democratic Party as conservative, and that change has made it difficult to predict or comprehend national election results in the years since that time.

On another point, we made no effort here to account for the dramatic increase in the number of "private academies" in the South since the Supreme Court decision in 1954, but it has been extensive. Such facts, however, would simply underscore the general reluctance of many people in Southern states to acknowledge the concept of "equality" as applicable to black Americans, even today. Increased financial support for the private academies, of course, has led to reduced financial support for public schools in the South, thus the task of helping young black males in the South, especially, to learn how to move from an "obedience" orientation to a "responsibility" orientation has been compromised still further. It is an intractable problem.

From Hope to Frustration and Aggression

The decade following the end of World War II—1945 to 1955—produced seeds of hope for black Americans after centuries of slavery, rejection, discrimination, and impoverishment.

Although the political accomplishments described below seem not to relate directly to black Americans, the fact that they occurred when they did gave clear evidence of the positive changes that were taking place in the political arena of the United States at the time: Kennan developed the "containment" policy against communism that America followed for the next 50 years; [10] the Marshall Plan was instituted to help European nations regain control of their economies; [11] the "Truman Doctrine" limited expansion of communism in Greece and Turkey; [12] Truman's Executive Orders 9980 and 9981 integrated federal workers and those in the armed forces; [13] the Berlin air lift assured Germans of American and English commitment to freedom; [14] the Korean War, supported by the United Nations, assured South Koreans of freedom and black Americans in the armed forces of full equality; Truman's election over one Republican and two Democratic opponents signaled the importance of freedom for all people; and the Supreme Court decision in *Brown v. Board of Education* promised equality of public education across all of America. [15]

1945 to 1955 were years of great significance for all Americans. The creation of certain public policies and the election of Harry Truman sent clear signals to all Americans (including members of the U.S. Congress and the Supreme Court) that freedom was important for all people and all nations, including *all* Americans. Hope was high across the land.

In 1948, President Truman issued Executive Orders 9980 and 9981, which eliminated discrimination throughout the federal government and integrated the armed forces of the United States for the first time in American history. Weeks later, Truman was nominated for president by the Democratic Party, but two others from within that party withdrew to run against him: Strom Thurmond, of the Southern Dixiecrat Party, and Henry Wallace, the Progressive Party candidate. Republicans nominated Thomas Dewey. Truman had three opponents to run against in the 1948 presidential election, and he carried the extra burden of rejection of his civil rights proposals by a majority of Southerners. But Truman was elected that November, to almost everyone's surprise. He defeated all three opponents, and came within two tenths of one percent of winning an absolute majority. His election triggered a monumental shift of public opinion among blacks in America that "the times, they are a-changin'." Hope finally emerged among blacks again, as it had briefly in the years following the Emancipation Proclamation in 1863, and during some of the years of Reconstruction. And hope revolutionized blacks in many ways.

One incident of that era is worthy of description regarding Truman giving hope to black Americans. Election day was just four days off. Philleo Nash who accompanied the president to Harlem, described the unusual behavior of the sixty-five thousand people in Truman's audience that day as follows: [16]

> *So I had my back to the crowd and when it was time for the President to get up and speak, after they'd had the ruffles and flourishes and invocation and a rather lengthy prayer, I heard—there was applause—and then I heard the CCNY [City College of New York] students saying and shouting, "Pour it on, Harry," "Give 'em hell, Harry," and then all of a sudden the cry wasn't being taken up by anybody and it was sort of fading away, and then they felt they didn't have any support for what they were saying, so they became silent, and all of a sudden, there was a big crowd, but a silent crowd.*

> *Well, this is rather ominous, rather frightening. I had my back to the crowd and I just wondered whether I'd been wrong in urging that this be done . . . So, I finally turned around and faced the crowd and then I saw why they were silent, it wasn't ominous. Almost everybody in that crowd was praying, either with his head down or actually kneeling. They were quiet because they were praying, and they were praying for the President, and they were praying for their own civil rights. And they thought it was a religious occasion.*

So that was my first real face-to-face indication of the depth of feeling that the people who were most intimately concerned with civil rights had about Mr. Truman, and I think ought to have served to a good many people as an indication of what was going to happen with the Northern Negro vote—well, with the Negro vote, because there wasn't much Southern [Negro] vote in those days.

Black Americans in New York city were hopeful that night. Hope is the fuel that drives ambition, and freedom enables those with hope to sustain human life at better and higher levels.

When hope exists, goals that might be realized are seen as opportunities for change. But opportunities are not opportunities unless perceived as opportunities. If opportunities are perceived as opportunities, however, individuals set goals or objectives for themselves that they could not even contemplate unless hope was palpable and real.

We have taken both time and space here to posit the notion of hope as an essential element in the hypothesis we are developing. For all practical purposes, hope was nonexistent in the lives of most black Americans from the early 1600s until the end of the Second World War. From the mid-1940s until the present day, however, hope has become more and more evident in the lives of black Americans throughout the nation.

But frustration also develops in the presence of hope and freedom. Without hope, frustration cannot exist, and hope was high across America following the end of World War II. Even black Americans had hope, for the first time since the years of Reconstruction, although the hope of the 1860s lasted less than a dozen years.

Hope is the essential precondition for thinking ahead and establishing goals, but absence of opportunity leads to denial of hope. "Hope springs eternal in the human breast" is simply not true unless opportunity also exists. Slavery denied opportunity, and slavery fostered dependent behavior, which often produced a condition that psychologists today describe as "learned helplessness." [17]

Learned helplessness follows directly from situations in which the consequences of specific behaviors are not predictable from previous experience: e.g., the unpredictability of how an overseer would respond to a specific behavior of a given slave. When the consequences of specific behaviors by those who enforced the conditions of slavery were consistent, slaves could learn to cope. They knew what to expect—punishment, forgiveness, reprimand, or whatever. When the consequences of specific behaviors by slaves were both erratic and unpredictable, however—one time the lash, the next time a reprimand, the next time the incident was ignored, and the next time extreme punishment followed—it meant that those who were punished were less apt to learn, less apt to know just what to do, even less apt to be obedient because the message from the overseer was neither consistent nor clear. Obedience usually followed, but hope disappeared.

With expanding opportunities, however, both hope and frustration manifest themselves in the lives and minds of those involved. Hope because opportunities imply possibilities that might be realized. Frustration because those same opportunities might be thwarted by circumstances or other people.

The frustration-aggression hypothesis was developed by John Dollard, Neal Miller, Robert Sears, O.H. Mowrer, and Leonard W. Doob in the late 1930s and early 1940s. Initially there was confusion about the hypothesis because of one sentence:

> *. . . the occurrence of aggression always presupposes the existence of frustration and, contrariwise, that the existence of frustration always leads to some form of aggression.* [18]

Stated this way, the hypothesis implied that frustration always led to aggression, and that was obviously indefensible. The hypothesis was then reformulated as follows:

> *Frustration produces investigations to a number of different types of response, one of which is an instigation to some form of aggression. . . . This rephrasing of the hypothesis makes the assumption that was actually used throughout the main body of the text. Instigation to aggression may occupy any one of a number of positions in the hierarchy of instigations aroused by a specific situation which is frustrating. If the instigation to aggression is the strongest member of this hierarchy, then acts of aggression will be the first response to occur. If the instigations to other responses incompatible with aggression are stronger than the instigation to aggression, then these other responses will occur at first and prevent, at least temporarily, the occurrence of acts of aggression. In our society punishment of acts of aggression is the frequent source of instigation to acts incompatible with aggression.* [19]

Hundreds of studies have been accomplished to test the frustration-aggression hypothesis. Without reviewing that extensive literature here, we will simply assert that, on the basis of a partial review, the hypothesis seems to us a reasonable way to help explain aggression in human behavior. With that summary explanation, we elected to include its central idea in our hypothesis to help explain high murder rates among black males in the United States.

Many blacks, especially males, have not yet "matured" (if that is the right word) to the point that they are able to comprehend the concepts and internalize the behaviors associated with becoming personally responsible as a human being. There are examples of these non-responsible behaviors everywhere. We cite only a few.

Note at the outset, however, that we are only talking about *some* black males, not *all* or even *most* black males, but *some*. Our guess is, (and it is a guess, as we said earlier), that maybe thirty to thirty five percent of adolescent black males are characterized this way. That is a significant number, but *not anywhere near most or all* of those who might be involved.

Stand outside almost any predominately black high school in center city of any large urban area and observe the students leaving school at the end of the school day. Note how many carry books home, suggesting they have homework that they must do. Note how many carry CD players, and have these musical devices "up and running" when they walk out the school house door. Almost no students take homework home.

Why do so few black adolescents take homework home from school? There are probably several reasons, but a primary one seems to be that they "don't want to be like Whitey." Their friends say exactly that: "Don't be like Whitey!" Black adolescents do not want to be seen as copying white students; such behavior will get them ostracized and criticized by their peers.

Peer pressure is a powerful force in the lives on young people everywhere. It almost looks like "obedience" to other people, but the pressure comes from inside the individual student rather than from some other person, as in the case of the "overseer" in the slavery situation or the "authority" in the experimental situation, which was described earlier. Further, "not studying" represents a willing acceptance of conformity to others' values and behaviors rather than a coerced obedience to one who holds power over the life and wellbeing of another.

College students who drink too much are conforming to "peer pressure;" they are not "obeying" their peers in any way. In exactly the same way, black males who are urged "not to be like Whitey" are conforming to expectations and values expressed by their peers, but in the process they are not learning to be responsible for their own behavior, either. Only peers could persuade a young black male that "book learning" and "studying" is not important in that young person's life, because those things are important. Listening to "rap" music may be enjoyable and easy; it is not a path to citizenship and respectability and responsibility. It's a "cop-out," and nothing more. It will not lead to understanding important issues or solving important problems or acquiring essential skills or enhancing one's employability. It only leads to wasted time and self gratification.

Research Regarding Responsibility

Our hypothesis assumes that obedience is premised on fear, and responsibility is premised on learning and understanding. Persons who are dependent learn to be obedient. Persons who are independent learn to be responsible. Responsibility is learned behavior, but it is always learned over an extended period of time.

Along that line, a moving statement by a young mother, black and single, who aspires to raise her son Jason to be a responsible adult, appeared in *Newsweek* magazine on July 19, 2004.

Studies show that African-American women have been outpacing our men in education and corporate America for two generations now. Almost half of black boys wind up a grade behind in school, and only a third of 20-year old black men are enrolled in college. All the more daunting is the fact that a majority of these boys and men were just like Jason, raised in a home by a single black mother. . . .

I am not completely awestruck at the fact that my son is only a couple of generations and a few miles away from poverty, crime, and abject desperation. He has no idea. Do I tell him? How? How much? He has to know eventually, for his own good. . . .

I talk to my mom all the time about raising a black man, and there's good and bad news. The good news is she did a pretty good job; the bad news is she's far from done, and my brother is 25. We worry that he moved to a bad neighborhood and may become a victim of crime or, worse yet, accused of one; that he isn't assertive enough at a job where he may be hindered by his race; that black women intimidate him; and that he'll be profiled by police because his pants are baggy.

Blessedly, there are great men all over the place who love and nurture Jason: my uncle, who drives 40 miles round trip out of his way each Tuesday to take Jason to the barbershop; my dad, who relishes getting it right with his only grandchild. And there are even books intended to coach me on issues like black male masculinity, peer pressure, academic achievement, the lack of fathers, and goal setting. But I still realize that at the end of the day, everything Jason is, everything he trusts about who and what he can become, will come from me. . . And then I get to the real work: I pray. [20]

Young people must learn about responsibility: what it is, how to assume it, what they must do to become personally responsible. Young people must learn to take charge of their own lives and their own behavior. Developing a sense of responsibility involves at least six things: [21]

1. understanding and accepting one's own abilities and strengths,
2. accepting one's uniqueness,
3. believing in the importance of doing more than is expected,
4. believing in the importance and fun of behaving responsibly,

71

> *5. understanding the power and possibilities inherent in exercising choice, and*
> *6. making intelligent decisions.*

First, their strengths. Almost every person has many strengths, even those who are seriously at risk. Almost every person can see and they can hear. They can walk and talk, think and feel, and they can relate to other people and to things. They can play, work, move about, and learn. They already have most of the attributes they need to do almost anything they want to do. They have abilities and strengths.

Second, their uniqueness. Every person is unique. Genetically, there are no two people in the world who are alike, except identical twins, of course. Experientially, every person in the world is different from every other person who ever was or ever will be. There are no two people who are alike in this respect. Different people can share experiences, but uniqueness means that one's abilities, strengths, and experiences enable each person to create a personalized set of learning circumstances; to achieve whatever that person desires. Each person is unique.

Third, doing more than is expected. If young people can learn to believe in the importance of doing more than is expected, they will have mastered a significant secret in life. Giving of oneself, going the extra mile, helping other people—all these things evoke both respect and commendation: from peers, from superiors, from subordinates, and from others.

Fourth, believing in the importance and fun of behaving responsibly. Being in charge of one's own life is more fun and more exciting than doing somebody else's bidding. Behaving responsibly brings excitement and enthusiasm into the life of anyone.

Fifth, understanding the power and possibility of exercising choice. Personal power is rooted in the opportunity to be in charge of one's own existence, one's own schedule, one's own priorities, and one's relationship with others. Choosing is the ultimate behavior, and making intelligent choices—the essence of meaningful existence in a democratic society—means simply that the individual can think things through, reflect, hypothesize, and then respond appropriately and effectively. Choices determine both the goals that people pursue and the means with which they pursue those goals, and making personal choices that are helpful to oneself and other people is the essence of responsibility. Understanding these things fuels motivation and helps young people move toward responsible behavior.

Sixth, making wise decisions (i.e., exercising choice in intelligent ways) gives people a sense that what they are doing is important as well as giving direction and meaning to their lives. Being responsible means, simply, assuming responsibility for one's own actions: setting goals, working to achieve those goals, evaluating efforts to achieve those goals, and starting all over again.

Learning to be responsible is important, but helping people assume responsibility is different from assigning responsibility to people. Assigning responsibility may result in a personal interpretation that obedience is required, which could lead to dependent behavior. Assumption of responsibility must be nurtured. The possibility of achieving independence must be realized. If young people can learn to feel responsible for who they are and what they do, then and only then will true maturity and a personal sense of responsibility be fully developed and internalized as learned behavior in the young.

The Nature of Responsibility: Children's Understanding of "Your Job" [22]

The marking of jobs as belonging to people—"yours," "mine," "ours"—provides for children an introduction to concepts of responsibility. The present study asks about the understanding children have of several implications to "your job," with particular reference to divisions of responsibility. Should you, for example, remember to do this job or can you expect to be reminded? Can you pass this job to someone else or should you do it yourself? Are you accountable if the job is not done? The study explores the extent to which children endorse some specific principles, and the nature of any developmental progression, within the context of household work—a context that is familiar to children and for which there are some available data related to the adult viewpoints children may encounter. . . .

One reframing could consist of taking a more cognitive approach, exploring the norms or principles on which judgments about responsibility are based. This is, for instance, the essence of discussion within philosophy and law about the circumstances under which an individual may be regarded as liable, blameable, or deserving of punishment. . .

An emphasis on liability, however, makes much of the philosophical and legal discussion remote from everyday life, especially that of children.

Exploring the distributive aspects of responsibility pays attention to these implications. . . . The present study considers three possible principles: (a) if you have created the need for work, you should attempt to fix it (others should not be asked to do so); (b) you should be self-regulating on jobs that are routinely yours, needing neither to be reminded nor to be paid; and (c) even if others agree to do a job that is usually yours, you still remain accountable.

In total, 104 [third grade] children were interviewed. . . All were [from Australia], and came from suburbs regarded as predominantly middle class.

The main results are threefold: (a) the three principles do not show the same age changes, implying that children do not acquire any one-dimensional sense of responsibility; (b) there is, nonetheless, a broad developmental progression; (c) it is clearly feasible to consider responsibility in terms of distributive norms.

Personal Responsibility Antecedents of Anger and Blame Reactions in Children [23]

A central developmental task for children is learning to control the expression of negative emotions such as anger. . . And . . . anger for the lay adult is effectively an attribution of blame. . . . A perceiver's moral judgment about a harmful event is affected by at least four dimensions of personal responsibility, which may be labeled: causality (did the perpetrator cause the harm), avoidability (could the perpetrator have avoided the harm), intentionality (was the perpetrator trying to produce the harm), and motive acceptability (were the perpetrator's motives acceptable or not). These dimensions were derived from analyses of jurisprudence and Heider's analysis of personal responsibility. . . .

Do children use these dimensions when making moral judgments? . . . . Children 5 to 15 years old received information about eight incidents of property damage that consisted of the factorial combination of avoidability, intentionality, and motive acceptability. After each incident, they then rated how naughty the perpetrator was, as well as how angry the victim would be.

In general, the interactions reported . . . indicate that the stories containing evaluatively positive information elicited higher anger than naughtiness ratings, whereas the difference was much smaller for stories that contained evaluatively negative information only. . . .

In general, the results bearing on the first three predictions are consistent with the notion that expressing anger essentially is giving a moral judgment. Results pertaining to the fourth issue suggest, moreover, that the use of morally relevant information might be seen as an important moderating influence on children's tendencies to become angry.

Legal Responsibilities of Students: School Officials Also Win Court Decisions [24]

School officials . . . win many lawsuits brought against them by students and parents, and the federal courts have delineated many legal responsibilities of students. Although students do have many clearly defined constitutional rights, educators' "lawsuit paranoia" is largely unfounded.

*These points were brought out by the results of a study I conducted of federal court decisions issued between the release of **Tinker** in February,*

1969, and the end of 1982. . . . First and foremost, students attending the nation's public schools do have clearly established legal rights protected and secured by the Constitution.

Students have a responsibility not to infringe other persons' rights to a school environment conducive to academic pursuits. . . . Students have a responsibility, even when engaged in the exercise of their rights, not to engage in violence and serious disruption of the educational environment. . . Students have a responsibility not to engage in conduct that can reasonably be predicted to result in material and substantial disruption of the school environment. . . . Students have a responsibility, even when engaging in the exercise of speech and expression, to attend classes and refrain from encouraging others to skip classes. . . . Students have a responsibility, even when engaged in constitutionally protected activities, to refrain from using vulgar, profane, and obscene words, and making libelous or slanderous statements about other persons . . . . students have a responsibility, even when engaging in actions involving speech, press, and expression, to refrain from acts of disrespect and insubordination.

Locus of Control of Children with Learning Disabilities [25]

This [locus of control] concept is derived from social learning theory and refers to the way in which individuals perceive sources of control over events in their lives; whether they perceive that reinforcements are contingent upon certain aspects of their own behavior, or somehow come by fate, chance, or other outside forces beyond their control. Internal locus of control refers to an individual's belief that reinforcement is a function of his or her own behavior. In contrast, external locus of control refers to one's perceptions of these same events as the result of forces such as fate, chance, or the actions of powerful others. Thus, some individuals see themselves as in control of the events in their lives, while others perceive these events as being controlled by fate, luck, or chance rather than their own efforts.

The purpose of the present study . . . was to determine whether the perceptions of parents and teachers regarding the locus of control orientation of their children with learning disabilities differed from the beliefs held by the children themselves.

The subjects were 24 white males between the ages of 8 and 12 . . . enrolled in self-contained classes for children with learning disabilities, their mothers and fathers, and their teachers. Twenty-six white males encompassing the same age span were randomly selected from the nondisabled school population, and together with their parents and teachers constituted the comparison group. . . The Intellectual Achievement Responsibility instrument was used to measure both the children's perceptions of their own locus of control and their parents' and teachers' perceptions of the children's [locus of control].

Significant differences were found between the nondisabled subjects and the children labeled learning disabled. Nondisabled subjects presented significantly higher scores (internality) for total [locus of control] and for positive (success) experiences. No significant differences were found for negative (failure) events. . . a significant difference was found between the teachers' perceptions and the beliefs held by their students labeled learning disabled. Teachers perceived their students as having a more internal orientation for success experiences than the students perceived for themselves.

Parent Management Practices and School Adjustment [26]

Some young people commit crimes, often of a violent nature. In 1986, just over 1.4 million arrests of juveniles for nonindex offenses (e.g., vandalism, drug abuse, runaway, etc.) were recorded in the United States. For the same year, 900,000 arrests of juveniles occurred for index crimes including larceny-theft, forcible rape, etc. . . . . At least 491,000 juveniles are incarcerated each year, with each one costing approximately $21,927 per year to maintain.

School officials report not knowing how to cope with or serve students with antisocial behavior patterns. In general, students who display antisocial behavior in school place severe pressures upon the management and instructional skills of their teachers. At school, these students are likely to experience major adjustment problems in the areas of academic achievement and peer social relations.

Patterson and his associates have developed an empirical explanatory base for the development of antisocial behavior patterns that centers around parent training and disrupted family management practices. They argue that children who enter school with an antisocial behavior pattern that is characterized by early onset, high rates, and occurrence in multiple forms and settings very often are the products of home environments where: (a) discipline methods of the parents are inconsistent and harsh; (b) monitoring of children's whereabouts, activities, and peer associations is infrequent and inconsistent; (c) positive family management including encouragement, social interest, and use of social reinforcers is lacking; (d) parental problem-solving skills are not well developed; and (e) parents are not involved actively in their children's daily lives. . . .

Each of the above parent management problems is conceptualized as a "construct" by Patterson and his colleagues. Four of these family management constructs, discipline, monitoring, positive reinforcement, and problem solving were tested specifically by Patterson and Stouthamer-Loeber in their study of the relationship between family management and delinquency.

The purposes of the present study were to validate further the school antisocial classification system outlined by Shinn et al. and to contribute to the body of knowledge regarding the relationship between parent management practices and antisocial behavior in the school. Specifically, this study contrasted the family management practices of the parents of subjects in the four school adjustment groups described above. . . .

Subjects in each of the four adjustment groups were compared on the five constructs measuring parent management style. . . parents of subjects of the Antisocial group scored the lowest of all four groups on the Monitoring construct. . . . When the four groups were compared on the Positive Reinforcement construct, parents of the Antisocial subjects again scored the lowest.

Perceived Childrearing Practices and the Development of Locus of Control [27]

A central assumption in developmental research concerning competence and control orientations is the hypothesis that such variables are learned through socialization by the generalization of contingence experiences. . . Because late childhood and adolescence are considered to be crucial for the development of conceptualisations of person-environment transactions, family education should be relevant for the development of locus of control orientations during this developmental period.

The predictive value of mothers' childrearing practices (data obtained from mothers and their children) for three aspects of children's domain-specific locus of control orientations is analyzed longitudinally. Childrearing practices refer among other things to parental reinforcement and punishment of the child's behavior and achievements, which are directly related to the child's experiences of contingency between its actions and their consequences.

Data about childrearing practices, obtained from the children, resulted in significant multiple correlations for the three aspects of locus of control: perceived childrearing practices explained 31% of the variance of internality, 24% of the variance of powerful others control, and 18% of the variance of chance control. Data from the mothers about their childrearing behavior predicted only internality in children's locus of control significantly (multiple determination of 20%), but not that of both aspects of externality. The relevance of late childhood and early adolescence for the development of locus of control orientations could be confirmed with longitudinal data.

The Achievement of Students in Low-SES Settings [28]

The national study, **Equality of Educational Opportunity***, reported that a child's attitude related strongly to school achievement, and that his or her self-concept and sense of control over the environment—or belief in the responsiveness of the environment—affected school achievement far more than family background or school characteristics. Coleman et al. suggested that an educational system must promote a strong sense of "self" in a child if he or she was to achieve academically within his or her potential. . . .*

Why do some children in a low-SES setting achieve when others do not? This was the broad question posed for this study. . . . this study sought to look at an extreme group (nonachiever) from low-SES homes and to compare them to the achiever, also from low-SES homes. . . . Locus of control was used to represent a personal self-attitude measure, and field dependence was used for a cognitive measure. . . . (N = 55)

Although there was considerable difference found between the achievers and nonachievers in their locus of control (p < .08), the stronger significant difference was found in the field dependence measure (p < .01) with the achievers being more field independent. . . . Consequently, if the results of this study were considered in isolation, the strongest predictor for failure by children from lower-SES settings would be those who (1) attribute failure to external forces, (2) are not analytical, and (3) are sensitive to social cues.

Japanese and American Children's Reasons for the Things They Do in School [29]

In research on why children achieve, one way of distinguishing among sources of motivation is to compare reasons "inside" the person with those that come from "outside" the person. Inside-the-person reasons have been variously categorized as internal, intrinsic, internalized, endogenous, and learning oriented. Outside-the-person reasons have been correspondingly referred to as external, extrinsic, exogenous, and performance oriented. . . . With regard to conduct, a third category of reasons becomes relevant. Children who are more **empathic***—whose approach to rules involves considering the effects of their actions on others—have been shown to be better behaved inside* *and outside the classroom than those who are more focused on punishments or rewards.*

A total of 184 American and 399 Japanese fifth graders participated as part of a larger cross-cultural project on socialization into rule systems. . . . Children were asked about reasons for adhering to norms in four broad areas of classroom life: academic performance (achievement), academic procedure, social procedure, and morals. . . . Sixteen specific issues were included in both countries.

As predicted, the repeated measures ANOVA for reason type revealed a main effect of country such that American responses were more external, averaged across domains and across action versus feelings questions. . . . American children were significantly more external than their Japanese counterparts within each domain as well as averaged across domains. Japanese children's relatively less external reasons for academic performance appear consistent with an image of Japanese education as generating internal motivation to achieve. In both countries reasons for action were least external for the domain of morality.

*When asked about reasons for action, either an open-ended "why" or a rating of possible reasons, Japanese children indeed showed less external reasoning than American. American children more often pointed to some external "carrot or stick," and they did so especially often when academic rather than social norms were at issue. In contrast, when asked about their **feelings**, Japanese were, on the whole, as external as Americans, and they were more external with regard to academic performance. These appear to be contradictory patterns. We believe that they are not, and that the mechanism involves motivation that flows from identification with adult authority. . . it is truly remarkable that where academic progress was concerned, nearly 30% of Japanese reasons for action, and an even more sizeable 40% of their reasons for feelings, concerned authority. In no area of classroom life did American authority responses even represent 15% of the total. Recall that this category was coded so as to exclude sheer punishment and reward and good versus bad grades. Thus, differences in its use serve to index an aspect of identification: a desire to please, or to avoid displeasing, the authority in question. . . . when (Japanese children) are asked, "Why is it important to do well on a test?" they readily say, "Because it means I've learned a lot." When they are asked a "feelings" question such as "Why do you feel good if you do well on a test?" they say, with perfect consistency, "Because my parents will be proud."*

Jack Frymier and Arliss Roaden

Children's Perceptions of Social Ability: Social Cognitions and Behavioral Outcomes in the Face of Social Rejection [30]

Perceptions of control and attributions about ability are reliable predictors of children's responses to failure on cognitive tasks. Children who attribute failure to relatively stable causes, such as lack of ability, often demonstrate a helpless behavior pattern following failure feedback in problem-solving tasks. They tend to see failures as insurmountable, persist less, and show deterioration in their problem-solving behaviors. Likewise, children who believe that intelligence is fixed (i.e., a stable trait) appear to prefer tasks that ensure success, and they seem intellectually debilitated when faced with difficulty. In contrast, children who believe intelligence can always increase with effort seem to seek challenges, persist in the face of failure, and recover readily following failure.

The present study explores the relationships between children's malleability and control beliefs and their responses to social failure. . . we hypothesized that children who believe social abilities are fixed (i.e., not likely to change much over time), and that social outcomes are beyond one's control and responsibility, would be predisposed to helpless behaviors (e.g., withdrawal, reluctance to participate) following rejection. Conversely, children who believe that social abilities and social fortunes are malleable and within one's control were predicted to be the most resilient to social challenges (e.g., show little negative affect, persist in social goals).

The primary hypothesis, that children's malleability beliefs and perceptions of social control and responsibility would be related to degree of helplessness following social rejection, was supported by the results.

Chapter 6
A Recommendation to Reduce Murder Rates

This has been a complex story. People have wondered why people kill other people since Cain slew Abel. Our analyses may even have complicated things still further. Trying to make sense out of so many variables in relation to one variable—murder—may have suggested complexities that are incomprehensible. We hope not.

Life is all we have. Life is important. Creating life, assuring life, maintaining life, enriching life, perpetuating life—most of what everybody in the world does is aimed at these kinds of goals. Farmers and physicians, newly weds and old grey heads, pilots and politicians, scientists, salesmen, truck drivers, store clerks, accountants: everyone wants to live longer, better, and with maximum joy in everything they do. Life is all we have. Life is important.

Every murderer has a motive—revenge, desire, frustration, jealousy, money, power—and the intricacies inherent in human beings and human relationships almost guarantee that things will sometimes go wrong. How people cope with those wrongs, when they occur, is a function of how people have learned to cope, because coping is learned behavior.

Pilots in training are taught to cope with emergencies—engine failure, stormy weather, and the like. Practicing what to do in an emergency helps pilots respond rationally and more effectively than they otherwise would. But training does not always help, of course, and plane crashes occur. The same is true for emergency personnel. Taught how to stop severe bleeding, they sometimes can and sometimes cannot get the blood flow stopped, and some people die. Learning not to drink and drive has saved people's lives—we will never know how many—but some people cannot seem to learn to drink and not drive, so drunken drivers still kill themselves and others every day.

Learning to cope with forces and factors that make up life is one way to reduce murder rates in the United States, but it is not an infallible methodology. Whatever we try, some people will still kill other people, for whatever reasons. Given our tentative understanding of what may contribute to high murder rates among young black males (i.e., the hypothesis described earlier), however, we feel compelled to make a modest proposal that we are convinced could lead to fewer murders among black males, and probably others.

The proposal is to increase and improve learning opportunities for incarcerated young men. Our wish is that young black males would learn more and better things about coping with difficult problems and being fully responsible while they are still at home and still in school, but we are not knowledgeable enough or skilled enough to suggest changes in homes and schools that we think would have any chance of being adopted. Our proposal, therefore, is aimed at those who establish and those who operate prisons: policymakers, in other words; and the guards, wardens, and those who comprise the operating staff of any prison.

Our proposal is very simple: increase learning opportunities for incarcerated prisoners. Our analysis suggests that young black males, especially, have not learned to be responsible for their own behavior. Reflecting on what we have learned in this study, we are convinced that many black males in America—given the cultural obsession of whites with obedience of blacks as a mechanism of control for so many generations—had neither the opportunities nor the time required to internalize the factual knowledge and the social skills essential to becoming a fully responsible human being. Incarcerating them in prison could be one step in that direction.

If incarceration is seen *as* punishment rather than a place *for* additional punishment, and if appropriate opportunities for learning are made a central focus of the incarceration experience, young black prisoners, especially, might be helped to acquire the knowledge and skills necessary to becoming fully responsible human beings. Most of them have not acquired that knowledge and skill thus far in their lives (they would not be in prison if they had), and though we can argue that "they should have learned that at home" or "they should have learned that at school," they did not. Understanding their home backgrounds or their school's way of operating might help us understand why they did not learn what they should have learned, but such efforts would miss the basic point: they did not get what they needed from their homes, and they did not get what they needed from their schools. Whoever is to blame is beside the point: young black males still need to learn to be responsible. Maybe prison can be a place in which they learn what they need to know.

We think that an educational program in a prison ought to be characterized in particular ways. First, it should be six hours each day, five days a week. Second, it should have four basic "courses," each 90 minutes in length (8:30 to 10:00, 10:00 to 11:30 in the morning, 1:00 to 2:30, and 2:30 to 4:00 in the afternoon). Each course should have a different emphasis or content: one should be *work-oriented* (e.g., using computers to maintain databases or create commercial art, auto mechanics, food preparation for hotels); *academics-oriented* (e.g., high school diploma, college diploma); *developing a sense of personal responsibility* (e.g., accountability, liability, honesty); and *understanding our social system* (e.g., government, history, court decisions).

The first two courses (i.e., work-oriented and academics-oriented) should be planned and taught according to conventional assumptions (i.e., scope and sequence, evaluation according to accomplishments and standards). The second two courses (i.e., developing responsibility and understanding our social system) should be taught to emphasize "big ideas" and "understanding" rather than whether the sequence of information over time makes a coherent whole or whether the learner demonstrates "mastery" or "competence." Courses three and four, more than courses one and two, must require students to grapple with the big ideas of our culture—honesty, liability, rights, responsibilities, state's rights, authority, power, influence, representative government, the role of police, judicial decisions, importance of valid information, importance of learning as a way of solving problems—thus the instructional emphasis should follow the pattern of most preachers rather than most teachers: one major idea every day, like a sermon, not necessarily related to what went before or what comes after. Each day of learning should be significant in its own right; it ought not to have to depend on what was taught yesterday or what will be taught tomorrow. And the emphases must be on *understanding* and "what this information means to me" rather than a test to be passed or a competency to be mastered.

We also urge that prison teachers be paid higher salaries than teachers in the public schools, and those prison teachers must be convinced that the unique approaches and methods required in courses three and four "make sense" to them before they begin teaching. Only that way will it be possible to attract some of the best teachers in the community to teach in the prison schools, and to get specific results.

We could illustrate this "prison curriculum" with many examples of "big ideas" that we think would be important for such prisoners to deal with—the *Constitution of the United States*, the *Dredd Scott v. Sanford* decision, John Stuart Mill's *Essay on Liberty*, Sissela Bok's book on *Lying*, Mark Twain's essay "From Bombay to Missouri," and Harriet Beecher Stowe's paper that quoted Alexander Stephen's speech about principles of the Confederacy, which were cited earlier in these pages. There are thousands of other such ideas.

And prisoners must also learn that those in power have not always done the right thing. Taney's decision in the *Dredd* Scott case is a classic example of a person in power who made a horrendous error, which affected us all. Jefferson's enthusiasm for "state's rights" is another example of leadership error that we still live with, producing different penalties for murder in different states or different procedures for voting in different states in presidential elections, even today. We all know, of course, that Nixon lied, but he paid the price. Others have made errors or committed crimes, but they were not always found out. The system does not work "perfectly" for the betterment of everybody every time. We know that. People make mistakes. But we have to keep trying to make the system work better, and it will only work better if each of us becomes a better person in everything we do. That applies to incarcerated prisoners, too.

There are those who maintain that prisoners cannot handle ideas such as these. That is precisely the point: most incarcerated prisoners today are under-educated, and states have an obligation (i.e., if they want to rehabilitate those prisoners and help them become decent human beings) to help them learn, and to learn, especially, the concepts and skills that are absolutely essential in a our kind of society. Responsibility is the core ingredient of democracy.

Neither regular teachers nor prison teachers should ever "teach down" to prisoners; they must help people raise their sights in terms of understanding and improve their skills in terms of interactions with other people. "Teaching down" will never help prisoners learn what they absolutely have to know if they are to take their place in society along with the rest of us. America is based on "big ideas" (e.g., freedom, equality), and responsible citizens must both comprehend and believe in those kinds of ideas if America is to become a better place in which to live (e.g., with reduced crime rates). Remember: more than a million persons were murdered during the past century alone. That is too high a price to continue to pay, even if it means that some young people will have to learn about some things that they never heard about before.

Various people will argue, of course, that this would cost taxpayers too much. People understand, however, that taxpayer's are going to pay the bill—anyway they figure it—before people learn to be fully responsible human beings by incarcerating them again and again, or by helping those people learn during their prison experience something besides how to be a better criminal (i.e., what they now learn from other incarcerated prisoners, with lots of spare time on their hands and nothing but boredom and insistence on obedience from prison officials).

Ignorance costs more than learning, and people who establish and operate prisons know that. If the public becomes aware of the kinds of "human costs" depicted in this study that involve people who are undereducated—high murder rates, high death rates from almost every known natural cause, low income for people of the state, high teenage pregnancy rates, and on and on—they will gladly pay the price. "Penny wise and pound foolish" is an admonition that fits problems related to crime and criminals perfectly, especially if the emphasis is on obedience and humiliation rather than responsibility and learning. It's time for a change.

Appendices

Appendix A
Voting and Citizenship Behavior:
Tables 1 and 2

PCREG60	Significantly more persons from low murder states registered to vote	1960
PCREG64	Significantly more persons from low murder states registered to vote	1964
PCREG68	Significantly more persons from low murder states registered to vote	1968
PCREG72	Significantly more persons from low murder states registered to vote	1972
PCREG76	Significantly more persons from low murder states registered to vote	1976
PCREG80	Significantly more persons from low murder states registered to vote	1980
PCREG00	Significantly more persons from low murder states registered to vote	2000
PCVOTE60	Significantly more persons from low murder states voted	1960
PCVOTE64	Significantly more persons from low murder states voted	1964
PCVOTE68	Significantly more persons from low murder states voted	1968
PCVOTE72	Significantly more persons from low murder states voted	1972
PCVOTE76	Significantly more persons from low murder states voted	1976
PCVOTE80	Significantly more persons from low murder states voted	1980
PCVOTE84	Significantly more persons from low murder states voted	1984
PCVOTE88	Significantly more persons from low murder states voted	1988
PCVOTE92	Significantly more persons from low murder states voted	1992
PCVOTE96	Significantly more persons from low murder states voted	1996
PCVOTE00	Significantly more persons from low murder states voted	2000

Table 1

Comparison of Mean Values for Those Registered to Vote
in 25 High Murder Rate States and 25 Low Murder Rate States with the "t" Statistic

Variables Registered	Table Addendum	25 High Rate States Mean	25 Low Rate States Mean	25 High SD	25 Low SD	"t" value
PCREG60	703	65.72	84.79	11.44	9.80	-5.233**
PCREG64	704	70.88	86.24	11.80	11.16	-4.170**
PCREG68	705	69.72	83.44	7.45	9.43	-5.382**
PCREG72	706	70.59	79.94	6.55	9.49	-3.912**
PCREG76	707	68.46	79.91	7.80	8.82	-4.772**
PCREG80	708	69.83	77.94	10.35	9.89	-2.769**
PCREG84	709	72.55	77.24	9.71	9.45	-1.694
PCREG88	710	71.08	75.64	9.27	9.95	-1.643
PCREG92	711	73.14	78.25	9.52	11.08	-1.719
PCREG96	712	76.54	79.85	8.59	9.22	-1.290
PCREG00	713	63.72	69.51	5.32	8.40	-2.879**

    *   Significant at or beyond .05 level of confidence.
   **   Significant at or beyond .01 level of confidence.

PCREG60	= Percent of voting age population registered to vote	1960
PCREG64	= Percent of voting age population registered to vote	1964
PCREG68	= Percent of voting age population registered to vote	1968
PCREG72	= Percent of voting age population registered to vote	1972
PCREG76	= Percent of voting age population registered to vote	1976
PCREG80	= Percent of voting age population registered to vote	1980
PCREG84	= Percent of voting age population registered to vote	1984
PCREG88	= Percent of voting age population registered to vote	1988
PCREG92	= Percent of voting age population registered to vote	1992
PCREG96	= Percent of voting age population registered to vote	1996
PCREG00	= Percent of voting age population registered to vote	2000

*** On the internet   http://www.fec.gov/pages/96to.htm

Table 2

Comparison of Mean Values for Those Who Voted in Elections
in 25 High Murder Rate States and 25 Low Murder Rate States with the "t" Statistic

Variables Voted	Table Addendum	25 High Rate States Mean	25 Low Rate States Mean	25 High SD	25 Low SD	"t" value
PCVOTE60	714	52.75	73.10	15.64	5.82	-6.099**
PCVOTE64	715	54.07	70.25	11.43	5.28	-6.428**
PCVOTE68	716	56.02	67.58	6.89	4.53	-7.011**
PCVOTE72	717	49.94	62.01	7.32	5.39	-6.641**
PCVOTE76	718	49.86	60.49	5.39	5.14	-7.143**
PCVOTE80	719	50.05	59.42	5.62	6.16	-5.619**
PCVOTE84	720	50.93	58.44	5.11	5.19	-5.153**
PCVOTE88	721	48.14	56.84	4.56	5.93	-5.182**
PCVOTE92	722	54.09	62.40	5.03	6.85	-4.987**
PCVOTE96	723	47.75	55.44	4.93	6.26	-4.826**
PCVOTE00	724	50.19	57.55	5.41	6.31	-4.429**

*   Significant at or beyond .05 level of confidence.
**   Significant at or beyond .01 level of confidence.

PCVOTE60	= Percent of voting age population who voted in presidential election	1960
PCVOTE64	= Percent of voting age population who voted in presidential election	1964
PCVOTE68	= Percent of voting age population who voted in presidential election	1968
PCVOTE72	= Percent of voting age population who voted in presidential election	1972
PCVOTE76	= Percent of voting age population who voted in presidential election	1976
PCVOTE80	= Percent of voting age population who voted in presidential election	1980
PCVOTE84	= Percent of voting age population who voted in presidential election	1984
PCVOTE88	= Percent of voting age population who voted in presidential election	1988
PCVOTE92	= Percent of voting age population who voted in presidential election	1992
PCVOTE96	= Percent of voting age population who voted in presidential election	1996
PCVOTE00	= Percent of voting age population who voted in presidential election	2000

***   On the internet   http://www.fec.gov/pages/96to.htm

Appendix B
Collecting and Expending Taxes:
Tables 3 - 9

PCLOCTAX	Significantly more taxes paid to local government by high murder states	1999
PCFEDTAX	No difference in taxes paid to federal government	1999
PCSTALO	No difference in per capita taxes paid to state and local government	1999
TAXRATE	No difference proportion of income paid in taxes to all levels government	1999
FED90	No difference in per capita tax and nontax payments to federal government	1990
FED91	No difference in per capita tax and nontax payments to federal government	1991
FED92	No difference in per capita tax and nontax payments to federal government	1992
FED93	No difference in per capita tax and nontax payments to federal government	1993
FED94	No difference in per capita tax and nontax payments to federal government	1994
FED95	No difference in per capita tax and nontax payments to federal government	1995
FED96	No difference in per capita tax and nontax payments to federal government	1996
FED97	No difference in per capita tax and nontax payments to federal government	1997
FED98	No difference in per capita tax and nontax payments to federal government	1998
STLOPP90	No difference per capita paid in state, local, and personal property taxes	1990
STLOPP91	No difference per capita paid in state, local, and personal property taxes	1991
STLOPP95	No difference per capita paid in state, local, and personal property taxes	1995
STLOPP96	No difference per capita paid in state, local, and personal property taxes	1996
STLOPP99	No difference per capita paid in state, local, and personal property taxes	1999
STLOPP00	No difference per capita paid in state, local, and personal property taxes	2000
STLOPP01	No difference per capita paid in state, local, and personal property taxes	2001
STAX90	No difference per capita tax and nontax payment rate to state government	1990
STAX91	No difference per capita tax and nontax payment rate to state government	1991
STAX93	No difference per capita tax and nontax payment rate to state government	1993
STAX94	No difference per capita tax and nontax payment rate to state government	1994
STAX95	No difference per capita tax and nontax payment rate to state government	1995
STAX96	No difference per capita tax and nontax payment rate to state government	1996
STAX97	No difference per capita tax and nontax payment rate to state government	1997
STAX98	No difference per capita tax and nontax payment rate to state government	1998
STAX99	No difference per capita tax and nontax payment rate to state government	1999
STAX00	No difference per capita tax and nontax payment rate to state government	2000
STAX01	No difference per capita tax and nontax payment rate to state government	2001
TOTAL90	No difference total per capita taxes paid to federal, state, local government	1990
TOTAL91	No difference total per capita taxes paid to federal, state, local government	1991
TOTAL94	No difference total per capita taxes paid to federal, state, local government	1994
TOTAL95	No difference total per capita taxes paid to federal, state, local government	1995

Table 3

Comparison of Mean Values for State Funded Expenditures
in 25 High Murder Rate States and 25 Low Murder Rate States with the "t" Statistic

Variables State Funds	Table Appendix	25 High Rate States Mean	25 Low Rate States Mean	25 High SD	25 Low SD	"t" value
STAPC89	G.472	1,471.48	1,665.36	871.50	502.51	-.964
STAPC90	G.475	1,560.88	1,741.44	797.51	508.98	-.954
STAPC91	G.478	1,649.86	1,827.20	830.42	571.22	- .880
STAPC92	G.481	1,744.97	1,981.46	1,002.59	574.50	-1.023
STAPC93	G.484	1,817.36	2,046.01	868.56	631.68	-1.064
STAPC94	G.487	1,953.09	2,166.60	1,018.85	637.02	-.888
STAPC95	G.490	2,057.08	2,209.66	803.03	669.71	-.730
STAPC96	G.493	2,165.92	2,267.85	718.41	730.04	-.498
STAPC97	G.496	2,210.93	2,402.15	714.80	788.50	-.898
STAPC98	G.499	2,340.81	2,476.49	718.67	873.59	-.600
STAPC99	G.502	2,456.54	2,630.07	808.81	904.78	-.715
STAPC00	G.505	2,460.49	2,744.68	729.57	889.10	-1.235

* Significant at or beyond .05 level of confidence.
** Significant at or beyond .01 level of confidence.

STAPC89	= Per capita expenditures of funds from state	1989
STAPC90	= Per capita expenditures of funds from state	1990
STAPC91	= Per capita expenditures of funds from state	1991
STAPC92	= Per capita expenditures of funds from state	1992
STAPC93	= Per capita expenditures of funds from state	1993
STAPC94	= Per capita expenditures of funds from state	1994
STAPC95	= Per capita expenditures of funds from state	1995
STAPC96	= Per capita expenditures of funds from state	1996
STAPC97	= Per capita expenditures of funds from state	1997
STAPC98	= Per capita expenditures of funds from state	1998
STAPC99	= Per capita expenditures of funds from state	1999
STAPC00	= Per capita expenditures of funds from state	2000

Table 4

Comparison of Mean Values for Total Expenditures
in 25 High Murder Rate States and 25 Low Murder Rate States with the "t" Statistic

Variables Total Funds	Table Appendix	25 High Rate States Mean	25 Low Rate States Mean	25 High SD	25 Low SD	"t" value
TOTPC89	G.474	1,699.97	1,972.83	795.02	496.94	-1.455
TOTPC90	G.477	2,059.55	2,210.90	1,025.85	516.25	- .659
TOTPC91	G.480	2,195.79	2,358.89	967.71	590.06	- .720
TOTPC92	G.483	2,381.50	2,590.19	1,146.25	586.92	- .810
TOTPC93	G.486	2,493.11	2,712.98	1,043.14	644.28	- .897
TOTPC94	G.489	2,701.10	2,878.48	1,216.93	624.82	- .648
TOTPC95	G.492	2,806.84	2,962.22	1,084.47	681.67	- .607
TOTPC96	G.495	2,919.73	3,050.80	913.49	744.73	- .556
TOTPC97	G.498	2,986.94	3,083.38	912.04	980.09	- .360
TOTPC98	G.501	3,155.39	3,292.61	905.51	868.24	- .547
TOTPC99	G.504	3,333.39	3,504.64	1,063.39	921.36	- .609
TOTPC00	G.507	3,419.10	3,701.12	1,146.88	898.42	- .968

* Significant at or beyond .05 level of confidence.
** Significant at or beyond .01 level of confidence.

TOTPC89	= Per capita expenditure of funds from all sources	1989
TOTPC90	= Per capita expenditure of funds from all sources	1990
TOTPC91	= Per capita expenditure of funds from all sources	1991
TOTPC92	= Per capita expenditure of funds from all sources	1992
TOTPC93	= Per capita expenditure of funds from all sources	1993
TOTPC94	= Per capita expenditure of funds from all sources	1994
TOTPC95	= Per capita expenditure of funds from all sources	1995
TOTPC96	= Per capita expenditure of funds from all sources	1996
TOTPC97	= Per capita expenditure of funds from all sources	1997
TOTPC98	= Per capita expenditure of funds from all sources	1998
TOTPC99	= Per capita expenditure of funds from all sources	1999
TOTPC00	= Per capita expenditure of funds from all sources	2000

Table 5

Comparison of Mean Values for Taxation Variables
in 25 High Murder Rate States and 25 Low Murder Rate States with the "t" Statistic

Variables Taxes	Table Appendix	25 High Rate States Mean	25 Low Rate States Mean	25 High SD	25 Low SD	"t" value
TABALCRV	G.253	41.59	46.81	15.43	15.52	-1.131
PCINCOME	G.347	26,561.64	27,947.88	3,530.97	4,513.34	-1.210
PCDISPIN	G.348	22,865.56	23,937.52	2,676.90	3,365.60	-1.246
PCFEDTAX	G.369	2,805.85	3,023.08	699.30	1,038.09	-.868
PCSTATAX	G.370	640.45	784.56	333.82	365.41	-1.456
PCLOCTAX	G.371	133.69	76.55	125.95	56.72	2.068*
PCSTALO	G.378	792.14	877.95	400.42	363.60	-.793
TAXRATE	G.376	.1337	.1370	.0167	.0193	-.649
PCFSLTAX	G.372	3,597.99	3,901.03	893.06	1,189.94	-1.018

*   Significant at or beyond .05 level of confidence.
**   Significant at or beyond .01 level of confidence.

TABALCRV	= Tax revenue, alcohol and tobacco, per capita	2000
PCINCOME	= Per capita income	1999
PCDISPIN	= Per capita disposable income (i.e., income after taxes)	1999
PCFEDTAX	= Per capita taxes paid to federal government	1999
PCSTATAX	= Per capita taxes paid to state government	1999
PCLOCTAX	= Per capita taxes paid to local government	1999
PCSTALO	= Per capita taxes paid to federal, state, and for personal property	1999
TAXRATE	= Proportion of income paid in taxes to federal, state, local governments	1999
PCFSLTAX	= Per capita taxes paid to federal, state, and local governments	1999

Table 6

Comparison of Mean Values for Federal Taxes Paid
in 25 High Murder Rate States and 25 Low Murder Rate States with the "t" Statistic

Variables Taxation	Table Addendum	25 High Rate States Mean	25 Low Rate States Mean	25 High SD	25 Low SD	"t" value
FED90	814	1,719.39	1,782.64	438.06	488.37	-.482
FED91	815	1,670.68	1,757.45	400.45	454.30	-.716
FED92	816	1,703.70	1,801.69	403.40	474.46	-.787
FED93	817	1,796.89	1,896.41	420.12	499.97	-.762
FED94	818	1,918.73	1,998.69	424.33	509.25	-.603
FED95	819	2,030.17	2,122.95	444.50	575.10	-.638
FED96	820	2,245.63	2,365.90	514.03	677.51	-.707
FED97	821	2,452.84	2,631.36	556.45	807.29	-.910
FED98	822	2,668.08	2,866.19	637.37	943.86	-.870
FED99	823	2,786.32	3,066.61	715.37	1,066.07	-1.092
FED00	824	3,007.48	3,401.28	824.52	1,275.68	-1.296
FED01	825	3.022.63	3,397.18	791.80	1,201.62	-1.301

*   Significant at or beyond .05 level of confidence.
**   Significant at or beyond .01 level of confidence.

FED90 = Per capita, tax and nontax payments made to federal government 1990
FED91 = Per capita, tax and nontax payments made to federal government 1991
FED92 = Per capita, tax and nontax payments made to federal government 1992
FED93 = Per capita, tax and nontax payments made to federal government 1993
FED94 = Per capita, tax and nontax payments made to federal government 1994
FED95 = Per capita, tax and nontax payments made to federal government 1995
FED96 = Per capita, tax and nontax payments made to federal government 1996
FED97 = Per capita, tax and nontax payments made to federal government 1997
FED98 = Per capita, tax and nontax payments made to federal government 1998
FED99 = Per capita, tax and nontax payments made to federal government 1999
FED00 = Per capita, tax and nontax payments made to federal government 2000
FED01 = Per capita, tax and nontax payments made to federal government 2001

Addendum and *** On the internet: http://www.bea.gov/bea/regional/spi/action.cfm
Computed: fed90 = fedtax90 / pop90

Table 7

Comparison of Mean Values for State and Local Taxes Paid
in 25 High Murder Rate States and 25 Low Murder Rate States with the "t" Statistic

Variables Taxation	Table Addendum	25 High Rate States Mean	25 Low Rate States Mean	25 High SD	25 Low SD	"t" value
STLOPP90	826	462.46	511.07	254.22	234.81	-.702
STLOPP91	827	486.87	549.99	259.69	241.88	-.889
STLOPP92	828	518.68	607.70	256.39	256.04	-1.228
STLOPP93	829	544.73	627.75	270.87	265.65	-1.094
STLOPP94	830	574.93	659.16	286.01	275.77	-1.060
STLOPP95	831	610.02	690.53	298.76	291.57	-.964
STLOPP96	832	645.57	732.61	310.00	311.31	-.991
STLOPP97	833	691.36	789.26	333.08	336.39	-1.034
STLOPP98	834	736.35	842.92	361.22	357.31	-1.049
STLOPP99	835	787.99	876.57	398.77	362.38	-.822
STLOPP00	836	830.85	927.42	434.57	388.69	-.828
STLOPP01	837	840.79	928.05	433.23	377.41	-.759

*   Significant at or beyond .05 level of confidence.
**   Significant at or beyond .01 level of confidence.

STLOPP90	= Per capita, state and local and personal property taxes	1990
STLOPP91	= Per capita, state and local and personal property taxes	1991
STLOPP92	= Per capita, state and local and personal property taxes	1992
STLOPP93	= Per capita, state and local and personal property taxes	1993
STLOPP94	= Per capita, state and local and personal property taxes	1994
STLOPP95	= Per capita, state and local and personal property taxes	1995
STLOPP96	= Per capita, state and local and personal property taxes	1996
STLOPP97	= Per capita, state and local and personal property taxes	1997
STLOPP98	= Per capita, state and local and personal property taxes	1998
STLOPP99	= Per capita, state and local and personal property taxes	1999
STLOPP00	= Per capita, state and local and personal property taxes	2000
STLOPP01	= Per capita, state and local and personal property taxes	2001

Addendum and   ***   On the internet http://www.bea.gov/bea/regional/spi/action.cfm
Computed: stlopp90 = (statax90 + loctax90 + pptax90) / pop90

Table 8

Comparison of Mean Values for State and Local Taxes Paid
in 25 High Murder Rate States and 25 Low Murder Rate States with the "t" Statistic

Variables Taxation	Table Addendum	25 High Rate States Mean	25 Low Rate States Mean	25 High SD	25 Low SD	"t" value
STAX90	839	.0252	.0270	.0116	.0117	-.550
STAX91	840	.0259	.0282	.0117	.0116	-.707
STAX92	841	.0263	.0296	.0111	.0116	-1.025
STAX93	842	.0268	.0297	.0115	.0116	-.894
STAX94	843	.0270	.0300	.0115	.0116	-.943
STAX95	844	.0277	.0303	.0119	.0116	-.778
STAX96	845	.0283	.0307	.0120	.0119	-.722
STAX97	846	.0290	.0318	.0123	.0123	-.802
STAX98	847	.0292	.0320	.0125	.0125	-.791
STAX99	848	.0302	.0323	.0132	.0125	-.566
STAX00	849	.0300	.0320	.0132	.0123	-.561
STAX01	850	.0296	.0311	.0129	.0118	-.439

*   Significant at or beyond .05 level of confidence.
**   Significant at or beyond .01 level of confidence.

STAX90 = Per capita, tax and nontax payment rate made to state government   1990
STAX91 = Per capita, tax and nontax payment rate made to state government   1991
STAX92 = Per capita, tax and nontax payment rate made to state government   1992
STAX93 = Per capita, tax and nontax payment rate made to state government   1993
STAX94 = Per capita, tax and nontax payment rate made to state government   1994
STAX95 = Per capita, tax and nontax payment rate made to state government   1995
STAX96 = Per capita, tax and nontax payment rate made to state government   1996
STAX97 = Per capita, tax and nontax payment rate made to state government   1997
STAX98 = Per capita, tax and nontax payment rate made to state government   1998
STAX99 = Per capita, tax and nontax payment rate made to state government   1999
STAX00 = Per capita, tax and nontax payment rate made to state government   2000
STAX01 = Per capita, tax and nontax payment rate made to state government   2001

Addendum and   ***   On the internet: http://www.bea.gov/bea/regional/spi/action.cfm
Computed: stax90 = stlopp90 / pcinc90

Table 9

Comparison of Mean Values for Total Taxes Paid
in 25 High Murder Rate States and 25 Low Murder Rate States with the "t" Statistic

Variables Total Tax	Table Addendum	25 High Rate States Mean	25 Low Rate States Mean	25 High SD	25 Low SD	"t" value
TOTAL90	853	2,181.85	2,293.70	555.28	559.21	-.710
TOTAL91	854	2,157.55	2,307.45	519.23	545.42	-.995
TOTAL92	855	2,222.38	2,409.40	513.05	593.81	-1.192
TOTAL93	856	2,341.62	2,524.16	535.44	622.19	-1.112
TOTAL94	857	2,493.66	2,657.85	550.37	642.83	-.943
TOTAL96	859	2,891.20	3,098.51	641.21	814.36	-1.000
TOTAL97	860	3,144.20	3,420.62	705.77	945.63	-1.171
TOTAL98	861	3,404.42	3,709.11	802.48	1,085.62	-1.128
TOTAL99	862	3,574.30	3,943.18	920.72	1,186.02	-1.228
TOTAL00	863	3,838.33	4,328.70	1,062.21	1,425.45	-1.379
TOTAL01	864	3,863.43	4,325.23	1,028.31	1,332.00	-1.372

*   Significant at or beyond .05 level of confidence.
**   Significant at or beyond .01 level of confidence.

TOTAL90 = Total per capita taxes paid to federal, state, and local governments   1990
TOTAL91 = Total per capita taxes paid to federal, state, and local governments   1991
TOTAL92 = Total per capita taxes paid to federal, state, and local governments   1992
TOTAL93 = Total per capita taxes paid to federal, state, and local governments   1993
TOTAL94 = Total per capita taxes paid to federal, state, and local governments   1994
TOTAL95 = Total per capita taxes paid to federal, state, and local governments   1995
TOTAL96 = Total per capita taxes paid to federal, state, and local governments   1996
TOTAL97 = Total per capita taxes paid to federal, state, and local governments   1997
TOTAL98 = Total per capita taxes paid to federal, state, and local governments   1998
TOTAL99 = Total per capita taxes paid to federal, state, and local governments   1999
TOTAL00 = Total per capita taxes paid to federal, state, and local governments   2000
TOTAL01 = Total per capita taxes paid to federal, state, and local governments   2001

Addendum and   ***   On the internet: http://www.bea.gov/bea/regional/spi/action/cfm
Computed: total90 = stlopp90 + fed90

Appendix C
Crime, Punishment, and Police Protection:
Tables 10 - 14

MURDER	Significantly more murders in high murder rate states	1998
ASSAULT	Significantly more assaults in high murder rate states	1998
RAPE	Significantly more rapes in high murder rate states	1998
ROBBERY	Significantly more robberies in high murder rate states	1998
BURGLARY	Significantly more burglaries in high murder rate states	1998
CARTHEFT	Significantly more automobile thefts in high murder rate states	1998
ASSAUL39	Significantly more assaults in high murder rate states	1960-1998
RAPE39	Significantly more rapes in high murder rate states	1960-1998
ROBBER39	Significantly more robbery in high murder rate states	1960-1998
BURGLA39	Significantly more burglaries in high murder rate states	1960-1998
MVT39	Significantly more motor vehicle theft in high murder rate states	1960-1998
ROBRATE	Significantly more robberies, per 100,000 population, in high murder	1998
ROBGUN	Percent of all robberies with a gun higher in high murder rate states	1998
ROBFIST	Percent of all robberies fist related higher in low murder rate states	1998
ASLRATE	Significantly more assaults, per 100,000 population, in high murder	1998
ASLGUN	Percent of all assaults with a gun higher in high murder rate states	1998
ASLFIST	Percent of all assaults fist related higher in low murder rate states	1998
MURPLOGV	Significantly more murders per person in local government in high	1998
PRISONS	Significantly more per capita expenditures for prisons in high murder	1989-2000
CRIMESPP	Significantly more crimes per person in state in high murder rate	1998
PRISPI96	Significantly higher operating costs per inmate in low murder rate	1996
FOODPI	Significantly higher food costs for prisoners in low murder rate states	1996
EXPT5069	Significantly higher executions, per 1,000 population, high murder	1950-1969
EXPT7700	Significantly higher executions, per 1,000 population, high murder	1976-2000
UTILPIPD	Significantly higher utilities costs for prisoners in low murder rate	1996
PRRATE92	Significantly more prisoners, per 1,000 population, in high murder	1992
PRRATE96	Significantly more prisoners, per 1,000 population, in high murder	1996
PRISENT	Significantly more prisoners, per 100,000 population, in high murder	1999
CORRECT	Significantly more per capita for justice costs corrections high murder	1996
JUSTCOST	Significantly more state local payrolls devoted justice system costs	1996
POLICOST	Significantly less justice payroll devoted to police by high murder rate	1996
CORRCOST	Significantly more justice payroll devoted to corrections by high	1996
JUSTEMPL	Significantly higher percent state local employees justice system high	1996
POLIEMPL	Significantly less justice payroll devoted to police by high murder rate	1996
JUDIEMPL	Significantly less justice payroll devoted to judicial and legal by high	1996

CORREMPL	Significantly more justice employees devoted to corrections by high	1996
JUSTRATE	Significantly higher rate per population of employees by high murder	1995
CORRATE	Significantly higher rate correction employees high murder rate states	1996
PRISON89	Significantly higher per capita expenditures to corrections high murder	1989
PRISON90	Significantly higher per capita expenditures to corrections high murder	1990
PRISON91	Significantly higher per capita expenditures to corrections high murder	1991
PRISON94	Significantly higher per capita expenditures to corrections high murder	1994
PRISON95	Significantly higher per capita expenditures to corrections high murder	1995
PRISON96	Significantly higher per capita expenditures to corrections high murder	1996
PRISON97	Significantly higher per capita expenditures to corrections high murder	1997
PRISON98	Significantly higher per capita expenditures to corrections high murder	1998
ASLKNIFE	No difference assault with knife between more or less violent states	1998
BURDENPR	No difference cost per person to fund prisons between more or less	1996-1999
JUSTICE	No difference per capita expenditures for justice systems	1996
POLICE	No difference per capita expenditures for police protection	1996
CORRECT	No difference per capita expenditures for corrections	1996
JUSTCOST	No difference percent justice payrolls devoted judicial and legal costs	1996
JUDIRATE	No difference rate per 10,000 population judicial and legal employees	1996
PRISON00	No difference per capita expenditures to corrections	2000

Table 10

Comparison of Mean Values for Various Crime Variables
in 25 High Murder Rate States and 25 Low Murder Rate States with the "t" Statistic

Variables Crime	Table Appendix	25 High Rate States Mean	25 Low Rate States Mean	25 High SD	25 Low SD	"t" value
MURDER	G.12	.08	.03	.02	.01	10.042**
ASSAULT	G.13	4.01	2.09	1.40	1.13	5.347**
RAPE	G.14	.39	.31	.11	.12	2.586**
ROBBERY	G.15	1.71	.78	.59	.55	5.800**
BURGLARY	G.17	9.84	6.80	2.45	1.67	5.118**
LARCENY	G.18	29.29	26.40	5.51	6.79	1.654
CARTHEFT	G.19	4.87	3.11	1.60	1.39	4.151**
ASSAUL39	G.280	289.36	140.97	82.44	63.18	7.143**
RAPE39	G.272	30.95	21.03	8.40	7.83	4.321**
ROBBER39	G.276	163.09	72.07	95.99	51.36	4.180**
BURGLA39	G.284	1,137.47	861.53	274.26	272.64	3.568**
LARCEN39	G.288	2,477.45	2,335.36	598.00	624.26	.822
MVT39	G.292	405.63	312.94	149.64	180.14	1.979*

*   Significant at or beyond .05 level of confidence.
**   Significant at or beyond .01 level of confidence.

MURDER	= Murder rate per 1,000 population	1998
ASSAULT	= Assault rate per 1,000 population	1998
RAPE	= Rape rate per 1,000 population	1998
ROBBERY	= Robbery rate per 1,000 population	1998
BURGLARY	= Burglary rate per 1,000 population	1998
LARCENY	= Larceny rate per 1,000 population	1998
CARTHEFT	= Auto theft rate per 1,000 population	1998
MURDER39	= Average murder rate per 100,000 population over 39 years	1960-1998
ASSAUL39	= Average assault rate per 100,000 population over 39 years	1960-1998
RAPE39	= Average rape rate per 100,000 population over 39 years	1960-1998
ROBBER39	= Average robbery rate per 100,000 population over 39 years	1960-1998
BURGLA39	= Average burglary rate per 100,000 population over 39 years	1960-1998
LARCEN39	= Average larceny rate per 100,000 population over 39 years	1960-1998
MVT39	= average motor vehicle theft rate per 100,000 over 39 years	1960-1998

Table 11

Comparison of Mean Values for Other Crime Variables
in 25 High Murder Rate States and 25 Low Murder Rate States with the "t" Statistic

Variables Crime	Table Appendix	25 High Rate States Mean	25 Low Rate States Mean	25 High SD	25 Low SD	"t" value
ROBRATE	G.402	165.52	75.37	60.99	54.50	5.551**
ROBGUN	G.403	44.80	30.04	7.84	10.77	5.539**
ROBKNIFE	G.404	7.95	9.04	2.21	3.45	-1.316
ROBFIST	G.405	36.56	47.46	5.67	11.13	-4.292**
ASLRATE	G.406	402.91	206.17	145.83	116.45	5.271**
ASLGUN	G.407	21.96	14.99	5.96	6.84	3.838**
ASLKNIFE	G.408	18.70	18.24	3.61	4.78	.382
ASLFIST	G.409	26.08	33.80	9.81	12.56	-2.392**
MURPLOGV	G.58	.0019	.0008	.0005	.0004	7.803**
CRIMLOGV	G.66	1.26	1.18	.32	.83	.423
CRIMESPP	G.50	.0515	.0396	.0091	.0100	4.248**
PRISONS	G.680	93.42	73.92	38.30	25.07	2.130*

*   Significant at or beyond .05 level of confidence.
**   Significant at or beyond .01 level of confidence.

ROBRATE	= Robberies, per 100,000 population	1998
ROBGUN	= Percent of all robberies with a gun	1998
ROBKNIFE	= Percent of all robberies with a knife	1998
ROBFIST	= Percent of all robberies that were fist related	1998
ASLRATE	= Assaults per 100,000 population	1998
ASLGUN	= Percent of all assaults that were with a gun	1998
ASLKNIFE	= Percent of all assaults that were with a knife	1998
ASLFIST	= Percent of all assaults that were fist related	1998
MURPLOGV	= Murders per persons in local government	1998
CRIMLOGV	= Crime rate per person in local government	1998
CRIMESPP	= Crimes per person in the state	1998
PRISONS	= Average per capita expenditure for corrections	1989-2000

Table 12

Comparison of Mean Values for Corrections Variables
in 25 High Murder Rate States and 25 Low Murder Rate States with the "t" Statistic

Variables Corrections	Table Appendix	25 High Rate States Mean	25 Low Rate States Mean	25 High SD	25 Low SD	"t" value
PRISPI96	G.67	18,566.00	25,376.56	6,483.46	6,426.55	-3.730**
MEDICPI	G.69	5.83	6.84	2.69	2.44	-1.326
FOODPI	G.70	2.67	3.67	1.09	.97	-3.404**
PRISCOST	G.71	79.40	63.33	30.98	30.47	1.849
PRCH9296	G.73	26.18	23.15	20.20	13.84	.619
EXPT5069	G.75	.0045	.0016	.0040	.0016	3.375**
EXPT7700	G.76	.0034	.0010	.0036	.0027	2.690**
UTILPIPD	G.72	1.78	2.28	.59	.75	-2.634**
PRRATE92	G.63	3.34	2.00	.78	.95	5.490**
PRRATE96	G.64	4.18	2.44	.99	1.16	5.730**
BURDENPR	G.141	79.40	63.33	30.98	30.47	1.849
PRISENT	G.416	448.76	250.88	108.91	86.58	7.111**
PROBRATE	G.415	1,656.44	1,721.71	1,010.41	1,072.30	-.219

*   Significant at or beyond .05 level of confidence.
**   Significant at or beyond .01 level of confidence.

PRISPI96	= Operating costs per inmate, per year	1996
MEDICPI	= Medical care per inmate, per day	1996
FOODPI	= Food costs per inmate, per day	1996
PRISCOST	= Prison costs per inmate, per day, per person in the state	1996
PRCH9296	= Prison population change	1992-1996
EXPT5069	= Executions per 1,000 population in the state	1950-1969
EXPT7700	= Executions per 1,000 population in the state	1976-2000
UTILPIPD	= Utilities per inmate, per day	1996
PRRATE92	= Prisoners per 1,000 population in the state	1992
PRRATE96	= Prisoners per 1,000 population in the state	1996
BURDENPR	= Cost per person to fund prisons in the state	1996-1999
PRISENT	= Prisoners, state and federal jurisdiction, per 100,000 population	1999
PROBRATE	= Adults on probation, state and federal jurisdiction, per 100,000	1999

Table 13

Comparison of Mean Values for Justice Variables
in 25 High Murder Rate States and 25 Low Murder Rate States with the "t" Statistic

Variables Justice	Table Appendix	25 High Rate States Mean	25 Low Rate States Mean	25 High SD	25 Low SD	"t" value
JUSTICE	G.381	362.02	317.13	124.76	79.41	1.518
POLICE	G.382	155.63	140.39	45.27	34.01	1.346
JUDICIAL	G.383	72.41	73.81	44.60	21.77	-.142
CORRECT	G.384	133.98	102.93	44.60	30.81	2.849**
JUSTCOST	G.385	12.57	10.90	2.91	2.54	2.158*
POLICOST	G.386	47.61	50.43	5.07	3.31	-2.326*
JUDICOST	G.387	19.41	22.46	3.16	4.74	2.675**
CORRCOST	G.388	32.97	27.11	4.98	4.42	4.395**
JUSTEMPL	G.389	11.83	10.05	2.08	2.30	2.879**
POLIEMPL	G.390	44.47	47.53	4.48	4.03	-2.540*
JUDIEMPL	G.391	18.61	22.18	3.72	4.33	3.129**
CORREMPL	G.392	36.91	30.28	5.10	4.23	5.002**
JUSTRATE	G.393	64.59	55.16	9.85	11.25	3.156**
JUDIRATE	G.394	12.04	12.40	3.11	4.43	-.336
CORRATE	G.395	23.97	16.74	5.56	4.02	5.273**

    *   Significant at or beyond .05 level of confidence.
   **   Significant at or beyond .01 level of confidence.

JUSTICE	= Per capita expenditures for total state and local justice systems	1996
POLICE	= Per capita expenditures for justice costs for police protection	1996
JUDICIAL	= Per capita expenditures for justice costs for judicial and legal expenses	1996
CORRECT	= Per capita expenditures for justice costs for corrections expenses	1996
JUSTCOST	= Percent of state and local payrolls devoted to justice system costs	1996
POLICOST	= Percent of justice system payrolls devoted to police protection costs	1996
JUDICOST	= Percent of justice system payrolls devoted to judicial and legal costs	1996
CORRCOST	= Percent of justice system payrolls devoted to corrections costs	1996
JUSTEMPL	= Percent state/local government employees devoted to justice system	1996
POLIEMPL	= Percent total justice system employees devoted to police protection	1996
JUDIEMPL	= Percent total justice system employees devoted to judicial and legal	1995
CORREMPL	= Percent total justice system employees devoted to corrections	1995
JUSTRATE	= Rate, per 10,000 population, of total justice system employees	1995
JUDIRATE	= Rate, per 10,000 population, of judicial and legal employees	1995
CORRATE	= Rate, per 10,000 population, of corrections employees	1995

Table 14

Comparison of Mean Values for Other Corrections Expenditures
in 25 High Murder Rate States and 25 Low Murder Rate States with the "t" Statistic

Variables Corrections	Table Appendix	25 High Rate States Mean	25 Low Rate States Mean	25 High SD	25 Low SD	"t" value
PRISON89	G.596	59.06	42.18	33.58	15.55	2.281*
PRISON90	G.603	73.49	50.59	45.46	22.21	2.263*
PRISON91	G.610	76.78	59.12	36.18	25.43	1.997*
PRISON92	G.617	80.08	64.22	45.74	28.81	1.467
PRISON93	G.624	78.27	64.79	34.63	26.54	1.544
PRISON94	G.631	84.49	64.85	39.88	24.01	2.109*
PRISON95	G.638	99.36	71.11	43.36	30.31	2.670**
PRISON96	G.645	102.15	79.36	37.41	35.34	2.213*
PRISON97	G.652	108.88	81.02	40.93	31.28	2.704**
PRISON98	G.659	116.74	90.42	39.83	35.14	2.477*
PRISON99	G.666	117.45	102.03	44.29	43.83	1.238
PRISON00	G.673	124.26	117.29	47.57	47.31	.519

*   Significant at or beyond .05 level of confidence.
**   Significant at or beyond .01 level of confidence.

PRISON89	= Per capita expenditures of total funds devoted to corrections	1989
PRISON90	= Per capita expenditures of total funds devoted to corrections	1990
PRISON91	= Per capita expenditures of total funds devoted to corrections	1991
PRISON92	= Per capita expenditures of total funds devoted to corrections	1992
PRISON93	= Per capita expenditures of total funds devoted to corrections	1993
PRISON94	= Per capita expenditures of total funds devoted to corrections	1994
PRISON95	= Per capita expenditures of total funds devoted to corrections	1995
PRISON96	= Per capita expenditures of total funds devoted to corrections	1996
PRISON97	= Per capita expenditures of total funds devoted to corrections	1997
PRISON98	= Per capita expenditures of total funds devoted to corrections	1998
PRISON99	= Per capita expenditures of total funds devoted to corrections	1999
PRISON00	= Per capita expenditures of total funds devoted to corrections	2000

Appendix D
Demographic Factors:
Tables 15 - 16

PCMINOR	Significantly higher percent minorities in high murder rate states	1999
PCMAJOR	Significantly higher percent majorities in low murder rate states	1999
PCWOMFRM	Significantly higher percent women firms in low murder rate states	1992
PCBLACK	Significantly higher percent black population in high murder rate states	1999
CHRISTAN	No difference percent of population that is Christian	1990
JEWISH	No difference percent of population that is Jewish	1990
POPDENSE	No difference population density per square mile	1999
PCMINFRM	No difference percent minority firms per minority population	1992
NOIMMUNE	No difference in percent of children not immunized	1998
PCUND18	No difference in percent of population under 18 years of age	1999
PCOVER65	No difference in percent of population over 65 years of age	1999
PCHOME	No difference in percent of families that own their own home	1999
PERHOUSE	No difference in number of persons per household	1999

Table 15

Comparison of Mean Values for Demographic Variables
in 25 High Murder Rate States and 25 Low Murder Rate States with the "t" Statistic

Variables Demographic	Table Appendix	25 High Rate States Mean	25 Low Rate States Mean	25 High SD	25 Low SD	"t" value
METROPOP	G.203	72.38	63.04	16.64	23.58	1.618
CHRISTAN	G.205	53.80	52.73	11.62	14.29	.292
JEWISH	G.206	1.53	1.14	2.02	1.44	.773
POPDENSE	G.49	145.58	206.23	122.53	318.35	- .889
PCMINOR	G.51	28.76	14.49	11.21	13.76	4.020**
PCMAJOR	G.52	71.24	85.51	11.21	13.76	4.020**
PCMINFRM	G.55	2.17	2.40	.61	.99	-.991
PCWOMFRM	G.56	4.02	4.84	.74	.84	-.672**
PCLOCGOV	G.57	3.77	3.50	.36	.80	1.522

*   Significant at or beyond .05 level of confidence.
**   Significant at or beyond .01 level of confidence.

METROPOP	= Percent of state that is metropolitan	2000
CHRISTAN	= Percent of population that is Christian	1990
JEWISH	= Percent of population that is Jewish	1990
POPDENSE	= Population density per square mile	1999
PCMINOR	= Percent minority	1999
PCMAJOR	= Percent majority	1999
PCMINFRM	= Percent minority firms per minority population	1992
PCWOMFRM	= Percent women firms per female population	1992
PCLOCGOV	= Percent population in local government	1998

Table 16

Comparison of Mean Values for Certain Demographic Variables
in 25 High Murder Rate States and 25 Low Murder Rate States with the "t" Statistic

Variables Demographic	Table Appendix	25 High Rate States Mean	25 Low Rate States Mean	25 High SD	25 Low SD	"t" value
ABUSE	G.20	.0117	.0098	.0032	.0058	1.445
NOIMMUNE	G.21	.2244	.2016	.0333	.0488	1.930
PCUND18	G.31	26.14	25.49	1.79	2.08	1.174
PCOVER65	G.32	12.20	13.17	2.09	1.68	-1.812
PCBLACK	G.34	16.13	4.30	9.62	4.79	5.499**
PCHOME	G.37	65.49	66.46	5.44	4.49	-.689
PERHOUSE	G.38	2.63	2.62	.09	.15	.529

   *   Significant at or beyond .05 level of confidence.
   **   Significant at or beyond .01 level of confidence.

ABUSE	= Child abuse, per cent of population	1998
NOIMMUNE	= Percent of children not immunized	1998
PCUND18	= Percent of population under 18 years of age	1999
PCOVER65	= Percent of population over 65 years of age	1999
PCBLACK	= Percent of population that is black	1999
PCHOME	= Percent of families that own their own home	1999
PERHOUSE	= Number of persons per household	1999

Appendix E
Death Rates: Tables 17 - 23

WWALDEA	Significantly higher death from all causes in high murder states	1994-1996
WWCARDIO	Significantly higher cardiovascular deaths in high murder states	1994-1996
WWPNEUMO	Significantly higher pneumonia deaths in high murder states	1994-1996
WWACCID	Significantly higher accidental deaths in high murder states	1994-1996
WWMOTVEH	Significantly higher auto death rates in high murder states	1994-1996
WWSUICID	Significantly higher deaths from suicides in high murder states	1994-1996
WWHOMICI	Significantly higher deaths from homicides in high murder states	1994-1996
WBALLDEA	Significantly higher death from all causes in high murder states	1994-1996
WBCARDIO	Significantly higher cardiovascular deaths in high murder states	1994-1996
WBMOTVEH	Significantly higher auto death rates in high murder states	1994-1996
WBDRUGIN	Significantly higher deaths from drugs in low murder states	1994-1996
MWALLDEA	Significantly higher deaths from all causes in high murder states	1994-1996
MWMALIG	Significantly higher deaths from malignancies in high murder	1994-1996
MWCARDIO	Significantly higher cardiovascular deaths in high murder states	1994-1996
MWPNEUMO	Significantly higher pneumonia deaths in high murder states	1994-1996
MWACCID	Significantly higher death from accidents in high murder states	1994-1996
MWMOTVEH	Significantly higher auto death rates in high murder states	1994-1996
MWHOMICI	Significantly higher deaths from homicides in high murder states	1994-1996
MBALLDEA	Significantly higher deaths from all causes in high murder states	1994-1996
MBCARDIO	Significantly higher cardiovascular deaths in high murder states	1994-1996
MBMOTVEH	Significantly higher auto death rates in high murder rate states	1994-1996
MBDRUGIN	Significantly higher deaths from drugs in low murder rate states	1994-1996
INFMORTT	Significantly higher total infant mortality in high murder states	1997
DEATHOMI	Significantly higher deaths from homicide in high murder states	1997
DEATHIV	Significantly higher death from HIV in high murder states	1997
DEATHMV	Significantly higher auto death rates in high murder states	1998
PEDEATH	Significantly more pedestrian fatalities in high murder states	1998
PCFATCH	Significantly higher percent change in traffic fatalities low murd	1975-2000
DEATHADJ	Significantly higher death from all causes in high murder states	1997-1999
MALIGADJ	Significantly higher death from malignancies high murder state	1997-1999
HEARTADJ	Significantly higher death from heart disease high murder states	1997-1999
CEREBADJ	Significantly higher death from cerebral in high murder states	1997-1999
ACCIDADJ	Significantly higher death from accidents in high murder states	1997-1999
MVACCADJ	Significantly higher death from motor vehicles high murder states	1997-1999

HOMICADJ	Significantly higher death from murders in high murder states	1997-1999
INJURADJ	Significantly more injuries from guns in high murder states	1997-1999
WWDIABET	No difference in deaths from diabetes, white women	1994-1996
WWNUTRI	No difference in deaths from nutritional deficiencies, white women	1994-1996
WWDRUGIN	No difference in deaths from drugs, white women	1994-1996
WWALCOHO	No difference in deaths from alcohol, white women	1994-1996
WBMALIG	No difference in deaths from malignancies, black women	1994-1996
WBDIABET	No difference in deaths from diabetes, black women	1994-1996
WBFALLS	No difference in deaths from falls, black women	1994-1996
WBSUICI	No difference in deaths by suicide, black women	1994-1996
WBALCOHO	No difference in deaths from alcohol, black women	1994-1996
MWDIABET	No difference in deaths from diabetes, white men	1994-1996
MWNUTRI	No difference in deaths from nutritional deficiencies, white men	1994-1996
MWDRUGIN	No difference in deaths from drugs, white men	1994-1996
MBNUTRI	No difference in deaths from nutritional deficiencies, black men	1994-1996
MBSUICID	No difference in deaths from suicides, black men	1994-1996
MBALCOHO	No difference in deaths from alcohol, black men	1994-1996
DEATHS	No difference in death rate from all causes per 1,000 population	1997
DEATHALL	No difference in death rate from all causes per 100,000 population	1997
DEATHART	No difference in death rate from heart problems per 100 population	1997
DEATHCAN	No difference in deaths from cancer, all races	1997
DEATHCER	No difference in death rate from cerebral problems per population	1997
DEATHSUI	No difference in death rate from suicide per population	1997
DEATHDIA	No difference in deaths from diabetes, all races	1997
ANYALCOH	No difference in deaths from auto accidents involving any alcohol	1999
PCHELMET	No difference in percent of motorcycle deaths with helmet	1999
SELFADJ	No difference in death rate from suicides	1997-1999

Table 17

Comparison of Mean Values of Death Variables for White Women
in 25 High Murder Rate States and 25 Low Murder Rate States with the "t" Statistic

Variables Death	Table Appendix	25 High Rate States Mean	25 Low Rate States Mean	25 High SD	25 Low SD	"t" value
WWALLDEA	G.89	377.14	343.79	22.82	29.89	4.435**
WWMALIG	G.91	107.93	104.64	5.28	11.73	1.278
WWDIABET	G.93	10.85	10.35	2.18	2.48	.757
WWNUTRI	G.95	.58	.56	.17	.21	.251
WWCARDIO	G.97	128.75	111.97	13.40	12.90	4.511**
WWPNEUMO	G.99	10.42	9.18	1.85	1.19	2.837**
WWACCID	G.101	20.56	16.88	4.60	4.32	2.907**
WWMOTVEH	G.103	12.54	10.00	3.64	3.36	2.562**
WWFALLS	G.105	1.87	2.04	.31	.49	-1.524
WWSUICID	G.107	5.08	4.40	1.37	1.11	1.926
WWHOMICI	G.109	3.07	2.10	.87	.66	3.941**
WWDRUGIN	G.111	3.18	2.89	1.28	1.19	.809
WWALCOHO	G.113	1.00	1.07	.51	.39	- .503

*   Significant at or beyond .05 level of confidence.
**   Significant at or beyond .01 level of confidence.

WWALLDEA	= Women white, all deaths per 100,000, three year average	1994-1996
WWMALIG	= Women white, malignancy deaths per 100,000, three year average	1994-1996
WWDIABET	= Women white, diabetes deaths per 100,000, three year average	1994-1996
WWNUTRI	= Women white, nutrition deaths per 100,000, three year average	1994-1996
WWCARDIO	= Women white, cardiovascular deaths per 100,000, three year avr.	1994-1996
WWPNEUMO	= Women white, pneumonia deaths per 100,000, three year average	1994-1996
WWACCID	= Women white, accidental deaths per 100,000, three year average	1994-1996
WWMOTVEH	= Women white, auto deaths per 100,000, three year average	1994-1996
WWFALLS	= Women white, deaths from falls per 100,000, three year average	1994-1996
WWSUICID	= Women white, deaths from suicides per 100,000, three year average	1994-1996
WWHOMICI	= Women white, deaths from homicides per 100,000, three year avr	1994-1996
WWDRUGIN	= Women white, deaths from drugs per 100,000, three year average	1994-1996
WWALCOHO	= Women white, deaths from alcohol per 100,000, three year average	1994-1996

Table 18

Comparison of Mean Values of Death Variables for Black Women
in 25 High Murder Rate States and 25 Low Murder Rate States with the "t" Statistic

Variables Death	Table Appendix	25 High Rate States Mean	25 Low Rate States Mean	25 High SD	25 Low SD	"t" value
WBALLDEA	G.90	548.45	497.72	64.05	97.62	2.079*
WBMALIG	G.92	130.33	130.49	14.28	16.85	- .034
WBDIABET	G.94	29.39	30.61	6.40	5.30	- .614
WBNUTRI	G.96	.95	.60	.28	na.	1.211
WBCARDIO	G.98	203.07	176.11	32.83	33.70	2.584**
WBPNEUMO	G.100	13.01	11.81	2.07	2.98	1.396
WBACCID	G.102	21.78	18.49	4.58	4.62	1.891
WBMOTVEH	G.104	10.82	6.37	3.75	.51	2.015*
WBFALLS	G.106	1.17	1.30	.27	.57	- .605
WBSUICID	G.108	1.99	2.40	.47	.	- .842
WBHOMICI	G.110	10.96	8.76	2.87	2.92	1.538
WBDRUGIN	G.112	3.88	7.63	2.21	2.36	-3.020**
WBALCOHO	G.114	2.14	1.60	.90	na	.578

* Significant at or beyond .05 level of confidence.
** Significant at or beyond .01 level of confidence.

WBALLDEA	= Women black, all deaths per 100,000, three year average	1994-1996
WBMALIG	= Women black, malignancy deaths per 100,000, three year average	1994-1996
WBDIABET	= Women black, diabetes deaths per 100,000, three year average	1994-1996
WBNUTRI	= Women black, nutrition deaths per 100,000, three year average	1994-1996
WBCARDIO	= Women black, cardiovascular deaths per 100,000, three year avr.	1994-1996
WBPNEUMO	= Women black, pneumonia deaths per 100,000, three year average	1994-1996
WBACCID	= Women black, accidental deaths per 100,000, three year average	1994-1996
WBMOTVEH	= Women black, auto deaths per 100,000, three year average	1994-1996
WBFALLS	= Women black, deaths from falls per 100,000, three year average	1994-1996
WBSUICID	= Women black, deaths from suicides per 100,000, three year average	1994-1996
WBHOMICI	= Women black, deaths from homicides per 100,000, three year avr.	1994-1996
WBDRUGIN	= Women black, deaths from drugs per 100,000, three year average	1994-1996
WBALCOHO	= Women black, deaths from alcohol per 100,000, three year average	1994-1996

Table 19

Comparison of Mean Values of Death Variables for White Men
in 25 High Murder Rate States and 25 Low Murder Rate States with the "t" Statistic

Variables Death	Table Appendix	25 High Rate States Mean	25 Low Rate States Mean	25 High SD	25 Low SD	"t" value
MWALLDEA	G.115	625.65	556.32	50.80	43.62	5.177**
MWMALIG	G.117	154.42	142.92	13.44	16.36	2.714**
MWDIABET	G.119	13.30	3.10	2.20	2.64	.291
MWNUTRI	G.121	.55	.50	.18	.17	.825
MWCARDIO	G.123	223.91	196.03	26.88	21.76	4.030**
MWPNEUMO	G.125	16.06	14.03	2.85	1.73	3.038**
MWACCID	G.127	49.75	40.68	11.42	9.41	3.066**
MWMOTVEH	G.129	26.69	20.60	7.33	5.623	.299**
MWFALLS	G.131	3.82	4.10	.47	.85	-1.457
MWSUICID	G.133	21.56	20.39	4.86	5.19	.821
MWHOMICI	G.135	8.59	4.36	3.71	1.37	5.311**
MWDRUGIN	G.137	6.52	6.73	3.97	4.11	-.181
MWALCOHO	G.139	4.21	3.85	1.45	.99	1.026

* Significant at or beyond .05 level of confidence.
** Significant at or beyond .01 level of confidence.

MWALLDEA	= Men white, all deaths per 100,000, three year average	1994-1996
MWMALIG	= Men white, malignancy deaths per 100,000, three year average	1994-1996
MWDIABET	= Men white, diabetes deaths per 100,000, three year average	1994-1996
MWNUTRI	= Men white, nutrition deaths per 100,000, three year average	1994-1996
MWCARDIO	= Men white, cardiovascular deaths per 100,000, three year average	1994-1996
MWPNEUMO	= Men white, pneumonia deaths per 100,000, three year average	1994-1996
MWACCID	= Men white, accidental deaths per 100,000, three year average	1994-1996
MWMOTVEH	= Men white, auto deaths per 100,000, three year average	1994-1996
MWFALLS	= Men white, deaths from falls per 100,000, three year average	1994-1996
MWSUICID	= Men white, deaths from suicides per 100,000, three year average	1994-1996
MWHOMICI	= Men white, deaths from homicides per 100,000, three year avr.	1994-1996
MWDRUGIN	= Men white, deaths from drugs per 100,000, three year average	1994-1996
MWALCOHO	= Men white, deaths from alcohol per 100,000, three year average	1994-1996

Table 20

Comparison of Mean Values of Death Variables for Black Men
in 25 High Murder Rate States and 25 Low Murder Rate States with the "t" Statistic

Variables Death	Table Appendix	25 High Rate States Mean	25 Low Rate States Mean	25 High SD	25 Low SD	"t" value
MBALLDEA	G.116	937.73	785.74	139.26	185.12	3.231**
MBMALIG	G.118	215.46	203.04	37.13	38.49	1.049
MBDIABET	G.120	28.55	33.15	5.41	10.99	-1.462
MBNUTRI	G.122	1.34	1.10	.44	na	.516
MBCARDIO	G.124	311.74	253.49	57.67	54.76	3.336**
MBPNEUMO	G.126	23.61	20.94	4.36	3.72	1.685
MBACCID	G.128	58.74	50.36	13.99	12.18	1.852
MBMOTVEH	G.130	28.09	17.82	9.37	3.39	4.547**
MBFALLS	G.132	3.57	4.25	.82	1.06	-1.099
MBSUICID	G.134	13.01	12.94	3.20	3.56	.046
MBHOMICI	G.136	55.36	49.15	17.04	17.42	1.051
MBDRUGIN	G.138	10.61	20.08	6.55	8.24	3.465**
MBALCOHO	G.140	10.49	9.53	3.95	4.92	.523

*   Significant at or beyond .05 level of confidence.
**   Significant at or beyond .01 level of confidence.

MBALLDEA	= Men black, all deaths per 100,000, three year average	1994-1996
MBMALIG	= Men black, malignancy deaths per 100,000, three year average	1994-1996
MBDIABET	= Men black, diabetes deaths per 100,000, three year average	1994-1996
MBNUTRI	= Men black, nutrition deaths per 100,000, three year average	1994-1996
MBCARDIO	= Men black, cardiovascular deaths per 100,000, three year average	1994-1996
MBPNEUMO	= Men black, pneumonia deaths per 100,000, three year average	1994-1996
MBACCID	= Men black, accidental deaths per 100,000, three year average	1994-1996
MBMOTVEH	= Men black, auto deaths per 100,000, three year average	1994-1996
MBFALLS	= Men black, deaths from falls, per 100,000, three year average	1994-1996
MBSUICID	= Men black, deaths from suicides, per 100,000, three year average	1994-1996
MBHOMICI	= Men black, deaths from homicides, per 100,000, three year avr.	1994-1996
MBDRUGIN	= Men black, deaths from drugs, per 100,000, three year average	1994-1996
MBALCOHO	= Men black, deaths from alcohol, per 100,000, three year average	1994-1996

Table 21

Comparison of Mean Values for Death Variables
in 25 High Murder Rate States and 25 Low Murder Rate States with the "t" Statistic

Variables Death	Table Appendix	25 High Rate States Mean	25 Low Rate States Mean	25 High SD	25 Low SD	"t" value
DEATHS	G.211	8.79	8.68	1.42	.29	.291
INFMORTT	G.212	7.97	6.55	1.20	1.09	4.371**
INFMORTW	G.213	6.40	5.96	.62	.95	1.931
INFMORTB	G.214	14.41	15.43	1.89	2.76	-1.293
DEATHALL	G.215	876.09	866.02	142.67	128.85	.262
DEATHART	G.216	272.35	261.19	61.08	56.54	.670
DEATHCAN	G.217	200.82	202.86	31.48	35.65	-.215
DEATHCER	G.218	60.62	62.06	14.12	10.17	-.415
DEATHACC	G.219	41.20	36.66	9.26	7.27	1.930
DEATHMV	G.220	19.83	16.11	5.87	4.67	2.476*
DEATHPUL	G.221	41.66	43.71	8.23	9.89	-.797
DEATHDIA	G.222	23.71	23.30	5.31	5.13	.279
DEATHIV	G.223	5.89	3.57	3.68	2.92	2.203*
DEATHSUI	G.224	13.01	12.75	3.74	3.61	.254
DEATHOMI	G.194	9.29	3.87	2.46	1.20	9.818**

    *   Significant at or beyond .05 level of confidence.
   **   Significant at or beyond .01 level of confidence.

DEATHS	= Death rate per 1,000 population	1997
INFMORTT	= Infant mortality, total, per 1,000 births	1997
INFMORTW	= Infant mortality, white, per 1,000 births	1997
INFMORTB	= Infant mortality, black, per 1,000 births	1997
DEATHALL	= Deaths rate from all causes, per 100,000 population	1997
DEATHART	= Death rate from heart problems, per 100,000 population	1997
DEATHCAN	= Death rate from malignancies, per 100,000 population	1997
DEATHCER	= Death rate from cerebrovascular causes, per 100,000 population	1997
DEATHACC	= Death rate from accidents, per 100,000 population	1997
DEATHMV	= Death rate from automobile accidents, per 100,000 population	1997
DEATHPUL	= Death rate from pulmonary problems, per 100,000 population	1997
DEATHDIA	= Death rate from diabetes, per 100,000 population	1997
DEATHIV	= Death rate from hormone immune deficiency, per 100,000 population	1997
DEATHSUI	= Death rate from suicide, per 100,000 population	1997
DEATHOMI	= Death rate from homicide, per 100,000 population	1997

Table 22

Comparison of Mean Values for Death Variables
in 25 High Murder Rate States and 25 Low Murder Rate States with the "t" Statistic

Variables Death	Table Addendum	25 High Rate States Mean	25 Low Rate States Mean	25 High SD	25 Low SD	"t" value
DEAGEADJ	868	900.55	810.62	71.67	59.87	4.815**
MALIGADJ	874	201.54	190.69	14.74	16.91	2.420*
DIABADJ	877	26.48	24.42	5.07	4.65	1.498
HEARTADJ	883	258.74	217.30	32.17	28.11	4.851**
CEREBADJ	886	61.55	55.98	9.00	6.22	2.546*
LOWREADJ	892	46.83	44.37	6.18	8.93	1.134
ACCIDADJ	901	41.88	36.33	9.68	7.71	2.245*
MVACCADJ	904	18.53	15.28	4.86	5.02	2.329*
SELFADJ	907	12.21	12.20	3.05	3.20	.018
HOMICADJ	910	7.93	3.86	2.26	2.17	6.199**
INJURADJ	913	13.00	8.64	2.95	3.48	4.776**

*   Significant at or beyond .05 level of confidence.
**   Significant at or beyond .01 level of confidence.

DEAGEADJ	= Rate of deaths per 100,000, all causes, age adjusted	2001
MALIGADJ	= Rate of deaths per 100,000, malignant neoplasm, age adjusted	2001
DIABADJ	= Rate of deaths per 100,000, diabetes mellitus, age adjusted	2001
HEARTADJ	= Rate of deaths per 100,000, diseases of the heart, age adjusted	2001
CEREBADJ	= Rate of deaths per 100,000, cerebrovascular diseases, age adj	2001
LOWREADJ	= Rate of deaths per 100,000, lower respiratory diseases, age adj	2001
ACCIDADJ	= Rate of deaths per 100,000, accidents, age adjusted	2001
MVACCADJ	= Rate of deaths per 100,000, motor vehicle accidents, age adjust	2001
SELFADJ	= Rate of deaths per 100,000, suicide, age adjusted	2001
HOMICADJ	= Rate of deaths per 100,000, homicide, age adjusted	2001
INJURADJ	= Rate of injuries by firearms per 100,000, age adjusted	2001

Table 23

Comparison of Mean Values for Highway Fatality Variables
in 25 High Murder Rate States and 25 Low Murder Rate States with the "t" Statistic

Variables Fatalities	Table Appendix	25 High Rate States Mean	25 Low Rate States Mean	25 High SD	25 Low SD	"t" value
FATALPOP	G.343	18.89	15.81	6.09	6.86	1.682
FATALCOH	G.189	37.96	39.96	6.52	7.36	- 1.016
TRAFATPT	G.193	.19	.16	.06	.06	1.878
PEDEATH	G.339	1.98	1.28	.73	.54	3.869**
ANYALCOH	G.342	37.80	39.40	6.73	6.12	-.879
PCFATCH	G.345	4.72	-17.76	28.73	16.48	3.394**
NOBELT	G.346	52.24	55.64	9.03	9.20	- 1.210
PCHELMET	G.380	50.82	43.75	27.58	27.78	.903

* Significant at or beyond .05 level of confidence.
** Significant at or beyond .01 level of confidence.

FATALPOP	= Traffic fatalities per 100,000 population		1999
FATALCOH	= Percent fatal accidents involved alcohol		1998
TRAFATPT	= Traffic fatalities per 1,000 population		1998
ALCOHOPC	= Alcohol consumption per capita, in gallons		1998
PEDEATH	= Pedestrian fatalities per 100,000 population		1999
ANYALCOH	= Percent of total traffic fatalities in which any alcohol involved		1999
PCFATCH	= Percent change in traffic fatalities over 25 year period		1975-1999
NOBELT	= Percent passenger car occupants killed, wore no seat belt		1999
PCHELMET	= Percent of motorcycle deaths with helmet		1999

Appendix F
Teenager's Social Problems:
Tables 24 - 25

LOWBIRWT	Significantly more children born low birth weight in high murder states	1998
TEENBRTH	Significantly more children born to unmarried teens in high murder states	1998
UNMARRBR	Significantly more children born to unmarried females in high murder	1998
TOTALBR	Significantly higher birth rates for females ages 15-19 in high murder	1996
NHWHBR	Significantly higher birth rates non-Hispanic females 15-19 in high murder	1996
NHWPCUN	Significantly higher births unmarried non-Hispanic white teens low murder	1996
HISPPCUN	Significantly higher births unmarried Hispanic teens in low murder states	1996
SMOK9596	Significantly higher teen births to mothers who smoked in low murder	1992
LACKINSF	Significantly more females age 12-19 lack health insurance high murder	1995
LACKINSM	Significantly more males age 12-19 lack health insurance in high murder	1995
BRYT96	Significantly higher birth rates teens ages 15-17 in high murder states	1996
PCTBRB96	Significantly more teen repeat births in high murder states	1996
PCTBAL96	Significantly more teen births as percent of all births in high murder states	1996
GONTEEN	Significantly higher gonorrhea rate females ages 15-19 high murder states	1996
BLACKBR	No difference in birth rates for black teens ages 15-19	1996
NHBPCUN	No difference in birth rates for unmarried non-Hispanic black teens	1996
NWHPCINC	No difference in percent teen births inadequate prenatal care	1996
ABORT95	No difference in teenage abortion rate per 1,000	1992-1995
PCCBR96	No difference in percent change in birthrates per females ages 15-19	1991-1996

Table 24

Comparison of Mean Values for Teenage Problems Variables
in 25 High Murder Rate States and 25 Low Murder Rate States with the "t" Statistic

Variables Problems	Table Appendix	25 High Rate States Mean	25 Low Rate States Mean	25 High SD	25 Low SD	"t" value
LOWBIRWT	G.207	8.12	6.90	.04	1.00	4.186**
TEENBRTH	G.208	14.87	13.62	1.12	2.04	2.686**
UNMARRBR	G.209	35.34	28.48	4.15	4.08	5.894**
ABORTION	G.210	19.58	16.12	9.75	8.30	1.349
TOTALBR	G.300	61.12	40.72	10.37	7.67	7.905**
NHWHBR	G.301	44.72	31.32	9.77	8.29	5.229**
BLACKBR	G.302	92.17	90.06	14.51	22.94	.356
HISPBR	G.303	98.43	111.18	28.20	15.06	-1.690
TOTPCUN	G.305	76.84	79.84	7.59	9.17	-1.260
NHWPCUN	G.306	65.88	76.44	9.85	11.38	-3.507**
NHBPCUN	G.307	95.20	94.06	3.58	6.06	.767
HISPPCUN	G.308	68.68	76.36	11.24	8.96	- 2.567**
TOTPCINC	G.309	10.24	8.88	2.54	2.59	1.876

*   Significant at or beyond .05 level of confidence.
**   Significant at or beyond .01 level of confidence.

LOWBIRWT	= Percent low birth weight	1998
TEENBR	= Percent of total births to unmarried teens	1998
UNMARRBR	= Percent of births to unmarried females	1998
ABORTION	= Abortion rates per 1,000 population	1996
TOTALBR	= Birthrate per 1,000, all females, ages 15-19	1996
NHWHBR	= Non-Hispanic white birthrates per 1,000 females, ages 15-19	1996
BLACKBR	= Black birthrates per 1,000 females, ages 15-19	1996
HISPBR	= Hispanic birthrates per 1,000 females, ages 15-19	1996
TOTPCUN	= Percent births to all unmarried teens	1996
NHWPCUN	= Percent births to unmarried teens, non-Hispanic whites	1996
NHBPCUN	= Percent births to unmarried teens, non-Hispanic blacks	1996
HISPPCUN	= Percent births to unmarried teens, Hispanics	1996
TOTPCINC	= Percent births to teens, inadequate prenatal care	1996

Table 25

Comparison of Mean Values for Other Teenage Problems Variables
in 25 High Murder Rate States and 25 Low Murder Rate States with the "t" Statistic

Variables Problems	Table Appendix	25 High Rate States Mean	25 Low Rate States Mean	25 High SD	25 Low SD	"t" value
WHPCINC	G.310	6.80	6.64	1.63	1.80	.329
NHBPCINC	G.311	12.68	11.06	3.61	4.22	1.333
HISPCINC	G.312	14.60	12.68	4.52	4.08	1.520
ABORT95	G.313	22.45	19.41	18.02	9.10	.700
SMOK9596	G.314	17.09	24.83	6.55	6.98	-3.870**
LACKINSF	G.315	18.68	13.32	5.81	3.42	3.975**
LACKINSM	G.316	19.16	13.08	5.56	3.37	4.679**
PCCBR96	G.317	-12.48	-13.84	5.11	5.18	.935
BRYT96	G.318	38.28	23.84	7.60	5.69	7.606**
PCTBRB96	G.321	21.96	18.12	1.74	2.44	6.406**
PCTBAL96	G.322	14.60	10.72	3.03	2.19	5.192**
GONTEEN	G.319	882.96	300.84	402.94	331.79	5.576**

* Significant at or beyond .05 level of confidence.
** Significant at or beyond .01 level of confidence.

NWHPCINC	= Percent teen births inadequate prenatal care, non-Hispanic whites	1996
NHBPCINC	= Percent teen births inadequate prenatal care, non-Hispanic blacks	1996
HISPCINC	= Percent teen births inadequate prenatal care, Hispanics	1996
ABORT95	= Teenage abortion rate, per 1,000	1992-1995
SMOK9596	= Percent of teen births occurring to mothers who smoked	1992-1995
LACKINSF	= Percent females ages 12-19 who lack health insurance	1995
LACKINSM	= Percent males ages 12-12 who lack health insurance	1995
PCCBR96	= Percent change in birthrates per 1,000 females ages 15-19	1991-1996
BRYT96	= Birthrates per 1,000 younger teens ages 15-17	1996
PCTBRB96	= Percent teens that are repeat births	1996
PCTBAL96	= Teen births as percent of all births	1996
GONTEEN	= Gonorrhea rate per 100,000 females ages 15-19	1996

Appendix G
Education:
Tables 26 - 28

STALOCPP	Significantly more funding per pupil in public schools in low murder states	1997
TOTINST	Significantly more dollars spent per student in schools in low murder states	1998
AVRSTART	Significantly higher starting teacher salary in high murder rate states	1998
HSGRAD	Significantly higher percent graduated high school in low murder states	1999
COLLGRAD	Significantly higher percent graduated college in low murder states	1999
COLLEGPC	Significantly higher expenditures for colleges per capita low murder states	1997
LIBRARY	Significantly higher circulation by public libraries for low murder states	1997
AVRSALRY	No difference average teacher salary elementary secondary education	1998
SCHOOL	No difference per capita expenditures elementary secondary education	1989-2000
COLLEGE	No difference per capita expenditures for higher education	1989-2000
SCHOOL89	No difference per capita expenditures total funds public education	1989
SCHOOL91	No difference per capita expenditures total funds public education	1991
SCHOOL92	No difference per capita expenditures total funds public education	1992
SCHOOL93	No difference per capita expenditures total funds public education	1993
SCHOOL94	No difference per capita expenditures total funds public education	1994
SCHOOL95	No difference per capita expenditures total funds public education	1995
SCHOOL96	No difference per capita expenditures total funds public education	1996
SCHOOL97	No difference per capita expenditures total funds public education	1997
SCHOOL98	No difference per capita expenditures total funds public education	1998
SCHOOL99	No difference per capita expenditures total funds public education	1999
SCHOOL00	No difference per capita expenditures total funds public education	2000
COLLEG89	No difference per capita expenditures total funds higher education	1989
COLLEG90	No difference per capita expenditures total funds higher education	1990
COLLEG91	No difference per capita expenditures total funds higher education	1991
COLLEG92	No difference per capita expenditures total funds higher education	1992
COLLEG93	No difference per capita expenditures total funds higher education	1993
COLLEG94	No difference per capita expenditures total funds higher education	1994
COLLEG95	No difference per capita expenditures total funds higher education	1995
COLLEG98	No difference per capita expenditures total funds higher education	1998
COLLEG99	No difference per capita expenditures total funds higher education	1999
COLLEG00	No difference per capita expenditures total funds higher education	2000

Table 26

Comparison of Mean Values for Education Related Variables
in 25 High Murder Rate States and 25 Low Murder Rate States with the "t" Statistic

Variables Education	Table Appendix	25 High Rate States Mean	25 Low Rate States Mean	25 High SD	25 Low SD	"t" value
STALOCPP	G.22	4,889.76	5,553.32	1,037.35	1,273.29	-2.020*
TOTINST	G.23	3,605.40	4,079.48	516.24	592.63	-3.016**
SUPSERV	G.24	2,005.52	2,147.76	288.85	360.59	-1.539
AVRSTART	G.25	27,019.00	24,865.12	2,035.33	2,413.73	3.411**
AVRSALRY	G.26	38,173.28	37,211.72	4,406.85	4,685.09	.747
STUMEDIA	G.27	10.21	9.62	1.89	2.01	1.079
HSGRAD	G.243	82.38	87.07	3.66	3.62	-4.551**
COLLGRAD	G.245	23.24	26.14	4.08	4.63	-2.345*
ADAPP	G.247	6,421.36	7,057.96	1,404.96	1.431.58	-1.587
ELESECPC	G.258	1,008.88	1.095.52	237.13	141.52	-1.569
COLUNIPC	G.252	392.36	437.36	77.78	108.65	-1.684
COLLEGPC	G.249	5.04	5.70	.63	.88	-3.060**
SCHOOL	G.676	585.79	577.08	197.24	175.84	.165
COLLEGE	G.677	339.02	321.07	141.77	153.02	.430
LIBRARY	G.725	6.13	7.80	2.27	1.58	-3.015**

*   Significant at or beyond .05 level of confidence.
**   Significant at or beyond .01 level of confidence.

STALOCPP	= Average funding per pupil in public schools	1997
TOTINST	= Total dollars spent per student in public schools	1998
SUPSERV	= Support services spent per student in public schools	1998
AVRSTART	= Average starting teacher salary	1998
AVRSALRY	= Average teacher salary	1998
STUMEDIA	= Average number of students per computer in school	1999
HSGRAD	= Percent over 25 who graduated from high school	1999
COLLGRAD	= Percent over 25 who have graduated from college	1999
ADAPP	= Expenditures per pupil in average daily attendance	1999
ELESECPC	= Expenditures for public schools per capita population	1985-1996
COLUNIPC	= Expenditures for colleges and universities per capita	1995-1996
COLLEGPC	= Percent of state population enrolled in college	1997
SCHOOL	= Average per capita expenditure for elementary secondary	1989-2000
COLLEGE	= Average per capita expenditure for higher education	1989-2000
LIBRARY	= Circulation, per capita, by public libraries	1997

Table 27

Comparison of Mean Values for Elementary and Secondary Education
in 25 High Murder Rate States and 25 Low Murder Rate States with the "t" Statistic

Variables Education	Table Appendix	25 High Rate States Mean	25 Low Rate States Mean	25 High SD	25 Low SD	"t" value
SCHOOL89	G.592	408.49	386.60	173.32	131.44	.503
SCHOOL90	G.599	485.33	428.32	231.00	147.27	1.041
SCHOOL91	G.606	509.91	471.05	201.34	156.45	.762
SCHOOL92	G.613	519.78	522.68	228.65	197.27	-.048
SCHOOL93	G.620	530.14	532.80	193.79	168.57	-.052
SCHOOL94	G.627	556.66	557.11	195.62	187.63	-.008
SCHOOL95	G.634	596.82	576.30	225.16	200.29	.340
SCHOOL96	G.641	635.47	614.82	218.57	201.31	.348
SCHOOL97	G.648	646.37	635.52	198.90	252.67	.169
SCHOOL98	G.655	685.63	690.23	203.05	230.49	-.075
SCHOOL99	G.662	711.27	736.95	205.66	229.86	-.416
SCHOOL00	G.669	743.65	772.60	226.91	198.43	-.480

*   Significant at or beyond .05 level of confidence.
**   Significant at or beyond .01 level of confidence.

SCHOOL89	= Per capita expenditures of total funds elementary secondary education	1989
SCHOOL90	= Per capita expenditures of total funds elementary secondary education	1990
SCHOOL91	= Per capita expenditures of total funds elementary secondary education	1991
SCHOOL92	= Per capita expenditures of total funds elementary secondary education	1992
SCHOOL93	= Per capita expenditures of total funds elementary secondary education	1993
SCHOOL94	= Per capita expenditures of total funds elementary secondary education	1994
SCHOOL95	= Per capita expenditures of total funds elementary secondary education	1995
SCHOOL96	= Per capita expenditures of total funds elementary secondary education	1996
SCHOOL97	= Per capita expenditures of total funds elementary secondary education	1997
SCHOOL98	= Per capita expenditures of total funds elementary secondary education	1998
SCHOOL99	= Per capita expenditures of total funds elementary secondary education	1999
SCHOOL00	= Per capita expenditures of total funds elementary secondary education	2000

Table 28

Comparison of Mean Values for Higher Education
in 25 High Murder Rate States and 25 Low Murder Rate States with the "t" Statistic

Variables Higher Educ	Table Appendix	25 High Rate States Mean	25 Low Rate States Mean	25 High SD	25 Low SD	"t" value
COLLEG89	G.593	224.75	247.49	90.69	108.33	- .805
COLLEG90	G.600	270.30	275.15	117.23	128.08	- .140
COLLEG91	G.607	293.23	281.65	120.32	146.41	.305
COLLEG92	G.614	302.37	315.12	137.96	190.75	- .271
COLLEG93	G.621	302.65	298.82	128.48	153.95	.096
COLLEG94	G.628	326.70	308.86	151.23	161.62	.403
COLLEG95	G.635	346.84	309.68	170.18	155.41	.806
COLLEG96	G.642	383.99	329.16	181.91	160.54	1.130
COLLEG97	G.649	383.42	328.65	170.47	178.27	1.110
COLLEG98	G.656	402.81	369.86	173.59	186.34	.647
COLLEG99	G.663	392.92	384.77	184.12	199.35	.150
COLLEG00	G.670	438.25	403.57	200.63	207.88	.600

*   Significant at or beyond .05 level of confidence.
**   Significant at or beyond .01 level of confidence.

COLLEG89 = Per capita expenditures of total funds devoted to higher education   1989
COLLEG90 = Per capita expenditures of total funds devoted to higher education   1990
COLLEG91 = Per capita expenditures of total funds devoted to higher education   1991
COLLEG92 = Per capita expenditures of total funds devoted to higher education   1992
COLLEG93 = Per capita expenditures of total funds devoted to higher education   1993
COLLEG94 = Per capita expenditures of total funds devoted to higher education   1994
COLLEG95 = Per capita expenditures of total funds devoted to higher education   1995
COLLEG96 = Per capita expenditures of total funds devoted to higher education   1996
COLLEG97 = Per capita expenditures of total funds devoted to higher education   1997
COLLEG98 = Per capita expenditures of total funds devoted to higher education   1998
COLLEG99 = Per capita expenditures of total funds devoted to higher education   1999
COLLEG00 = Per capita expenditures of total funds devoted to higher education   2000

Appendix H
Employment and Work:
Tables 29 - 33

TRADEPC	Significant difference higher percent employees in trade in low murder	2000
FINANCPC	Significant difference higher percent employees in finance in low murder	2000
RETAILPC	Significant difference higher retail sales, per capita, in low murder rate	1997
UNEMPAVR	Significant difference higher unemployment benefits in low murder rate	1998
TEMPASST	Significant difference higher temporary assistance in high murder rate	1998
FOODSTAM	Significant difference higher food stamp program in high murder rate	1998
PERBELPV	Significant difference higher percent below poverty in high murder states	1998
BANKRPPC	Significant difference bankruptcies higher percent population in high murder states	1999
PCBELPOV	Significant difference higher percent below poverty in high murder states	1997
CHBELPPV	Significant difference higher percent below poverty in high murder states	1997
CHILDPOV	Significant difference higher percent below poverty in high murder states	1999
BANKRPPC	Significant difference higher percent bankruptcies in high murder states	1999
PATENTPC	Significant difference higher patents per population in low murder states	1998
COMPUTER	Significant difference higher percent households with computers in low	2000
CONSTRPC	No difference percent employees in construction	2000
MANUFAPC	No difference percent employees in manufacturing	2000
TRANSPC	No difference percent employees in transportation and public utilities	2000
GOVFSLPC	No difference percent employees who work for government any leve	2000
PCEMPCHG	No difference percent employment change	1990-1998
INSUNEMP	No difference percent unemployed who were insured	1999
AVRPAY	No difference average annual pay	1998
RDUNIPC	No difference research development funds allocated by universities	1998
MINERLPP	No difference in minerals income per person	1998
PCINC94	No difference per capita personal income (code 030)	1994
PCINC95	No difference per capita personal income (code 030)	1995
PCDISP93	No difference per capita disposable income (code 050) after taxes	1993
PCDISP94	No difference per capita disposable income (code 050) after taxes	1994
PCDISP95	No difference per capita disposable income (code 050) after taxes	1995

Table 29

Comparison of Mean Values for Employment Related Variables
in 25 High Murder Rate States and 25 Low Murder Rate States with the "t" Statistic

Variables Employment	Table Appendix	25 High Rate States Mean	25 Low Rate States Mean	25 High SD	25 Low SD	"t" value
CONSTRPC	G.143	2.59	2.57	.67	.66	.118
MANUFAPC	G.144	6.69	6.61	2.79	2.32	.120
TRANSPC	G.145	2.60	2.53	.53	.48	.472
TRADEPC	G.146	10.93	11.88	.95	.94	-3.561**
FINANCPC	G.147	2.49	2.97	.57	1.03	-2.015*
SERVICPC	G.148	13.99	14.74	2.99	1.66	-1.090
GOVFSLPC	G.142	7.91	8.21	1.19	1.25	- .883
PCEMPCHG	G.43	17.20	19.25	25.66	13.62	- .352
RETAILPC	G.44	9,109.84	10,048.56	816.46	1,675.85	-2.518*

*	Significant at or beyond .05 level of confidence.	
**	Significant at or beyond .01 level of confidence.	

CONSTRPC	= Percent of employees in construction	2000
MANUFAPC	= Percent of employees in manufacturing	2000
TRANSPC	= Percent of employees in transportation and public utilities	2000
TRADEPC	= Percent of employees in trade, insurance, and real estate	2000
FINANCPC	= Percent of employees in finance	2000
SERVICPC	= Percent of employees in service	1998
GOVFSLPC	= Percent of employees who work for government at any level	2000
PCEMPCHG	= Percent employment change	1990-1998
RETAILPC	= Retail sales, per capita	1997

Table 30

Comparison of Mean Values for Economic Variables
in 25 High Murder Rate States and 25 Low Murder Rate States with the "t" Statistic

Variables Economic	Table Appendix	25 High Rate States Mean	25 Low Rate States Mean	25 High SD	25 Low SD	"t" value
UNEMPAVR	G.150	181.40	209.64	32.23	34.40	-2.995**
WORKCOMP	G.151	1,079.16	466.20	1,489.12	535.72	1.937
TEMPASST	G.152	79.36	21.60	126.12	24.73	2.247*
FOODSTAM	G.153	559.44	162.88	474.34	169.37	3.937**
TOTUNEMP	G.157	4.32	3.91	.85	1.13	1.425
INSUNEMP	G.158	1.73	1.88	.83	.79	-.627
AVRPAY	G.159	29,787.32	28,796.80	3,992.36	4,573.67	.816
PCUNION	G.160	13.26	15.47	6.31	4.84	-1.391
MEDINCOM	G.39	35,291.88	37,650.28	4,620.85	5,200.99	-1.695
PCBELPOV	G.41	14.19	10.97	2.86	2.10	4.527**
CHBELPOV	G.42	20.89	15.67	3.95	2.96	5.290**
UNEMRATE	G.80	4.02	3.48	.89	.90	2.115*
CHILDPOV	G.250	17.81	14.89	5.99	3.77	2.063*

* Significant at or beyond .05 level of confidence.
** Significant at or beyond .01 level of confidence.

UNEMPAVR	= Unemployment weekly benefits	1998
WORKCOMP	= Workers' compensation	1998
TEMPASST	= Temporary assistance, in thousands	1998
FOODSTAM	= Food stamp program, in thousands	1998
TOTUNEMP	= Percent unemployed	1999
INSUNEMP	= Percent unemployed who were insured	1999
AVRPAY	= Average annual pay	1998
PCUNION	= Percent of workers who belong to a union	1999
MEDINCOM	= Median household income	1997
PCBELPOV	= Percent below poverty	1997
CHBELPOV	= Percent of children below poverty	1997
UNEMRATE	= Unemployment rate, percent, in July	2000
CHILDPOV	= Percent children ages 5-17 in poverty	1999

Table 31

Comparison of Mean Values for Other Economic Variables
in 25 High Murder Rate States and 25 Low Murder Rate States with the "t" Statistic

Variables Economic	Table Appendix	25 High Rate States Mean	25 Low Rate States Mean	25 High SD	25 Low SD	"t" value
INCOMEPC	G.162	26,460.16	28,050.24	3,487.05	4,447.41	-1.407
MEDINC98	G.165	37,678.12	39,621.52	5,563.05	5,876.90	-1.201
PERBELPV	G.166	13.32	11.08	3.32	2.55	2.674*
BANKRPPC	G.164	.55	.44	.16	.10	3.035**
PATENTPC	G.174	22.89	34.81	11.72	20.68	-2.508*
COMPUTER	G.175	39.99	45.34	7.13	6.69	-2.733**
INTERNET	G.176	24.56	27.56	5.99	5.28	-1.878
RDINDPC	G.179	583.05	809.48	455.32	772.51	-1.263
RDUNIPC	G.180	88.20	95.55	42.68	38.17	-.643
FARMINPP	G.195	172.81	323.64	139.56	420.62	-1.702
MINERLPP	G.196	276.92	230.78	427.61	398.70	.395
BUSFALPC	G.344	.21	.27	.12	.15	-1.591

*   Significant at or beyond .05 level of confidence.
**   Significant at or beyond .01 level of confidence.

INCOMEPC	= Personal income, per capita	1999
MEDINC98	= Household median income	1998
PERBELPV	= Percent below poverty	1998
BANKRPPC	= Bankruptcies, percent of population	1999
PATENTPC	= Patents per 100,000 persons	1998
COMPUTER	= Percent of households with computers	2000
INTERNET	= Percent of households connected to the internet	2000
RDINDPC	= Research and development funds allocated by industry	1998
RDUNIPC	= Research and development funds allocated by universities	1998
FARMINPP	= Farm income per person	1998
MINERLPP	= Minerals income per person	1999
BUSFALPC	= Business failures per 1,000 population	1998

Table 32

Comparison of Mean Values for Personal Income
in 25 High Murder Rate States and 25 Low Murder Rate States with the "t" Statistic

Variables Income	Table Addendum	25 High Rate States Mean	25 Low Rate States Mean	25 High SD	25 Low SD	"t" value
PCINC90	731	18,147.08	19,024.00	2,812.58	3,033.06	-1.060
PCINC91	738	18,654.20	19,531.40	2,737.01	2,966.69	-1.087
PCINC92	745	19,564.68	20,487.36	2,750.42	3,097.09	-1.114
PCINC93	752	20,220.00	21,072.08	2,740.75	3,135.69	-1.023
PCINC94	759	21,176.72	21,881.84	3,008.63	3,144.57	- .810
PCINC95	766	21,890.28	22,669.68	2,833.30	3,349.94	- .888
PCINC96	773	22,741.96	23,790.40	2,929.81	3,444.58	-1.159
PCINC97	780	23,749.72	24,800.00	3,053.84	3,773.06	-1.082
PCINC98	787	25,030.76	26,322.48	3,241.69	4,036.22	-1.248
PCINC99	794	25,837.04	27,278.92	3,454.79	4,271.54	-1.312
PCINC00	801	27,355.12	29,117.80	3,850.98	4,857.41	-1.422
PCINC01	808	28,059.24	30,007.76	3,827.25	4,835.92	-1.580

*   Significant at or beyond .05 level of confidence.
**   Significant at or beyond .01 level of confidence.

PCINC90	= Per capita personal income (code 030)	1990
PCINC91	= Per capita personal income (code 030)	1990
PCINC92	= Per capita personal income (code 030)	1990
PCINC93	= Per capita personal income (code 030)	1990
PCINC94	= Per capita personal income (code 030)	1990
PCINC95	= Per capita personal income (code 030)	1990
PCINC96	= Per capita personal income (code 030)	1990
PCINC97	= Per capita personal income (code 030)	1990
PCINC98	= Per capita personal income (code 030)	1990
PCINC99	= Per capita personal income (code 030)	1990
PCINC00	= Per capita personal income (code 030)	1990
PCINC01	= Per capita personal income (code 030)	1990

Addendum and   ***   On the internet   http://www.bea.gov/bea/regional/spi/action.cfm

Table 33

Comparison of Mean Values for Disposable Income
in 25 High Murder Rate States and 25 Low Murder Rate States with the "t" Statistic

Variables Income	Table Addendum	25 High Rate States Mean	25 Low Rate States Mean	25 High SD	25 Low SD	"t" value
PCDISP90	732	15,965.16	16,730.20	2,284.74	2,509.87	-1.127
PCDISP91	739	16,496.64	17,224.12	2,252.33	2,460.65	-1.090
PCDISP92	746	17,342.24	18,078.00	2,266.01	2,546.63	-1.079
PCDISP93	753	17,878.36	18,547.96	2,245.72	2,556.15	- .984
PCDISP94	760	18,562.96	19,224.00	2,230.01	2,557.17	- .974
PCDISP95	767	19,250.08	19,856.28	2,304.73	2,686.83	- .856
PCDISP96	774	19,850.76	20,691.96	2,329.97	2,699.86	-1.179
PCDISP97	781	20,605.68	21,419.32	2,397.08	2,870.91	-1.088
PCDISP98	788	21,626.20	22,613.28	2,487.66	3,006.28	-1.265
PCDISP99	795	22,262.64	23,335.20	2,598.19	3,135.70	-1.317
PCDISP00	802	23,520.00	24,789.20	2,864.30	3,499.72	-1.403
PCDISP01	809	24,195.88	25,653.72	2,858.07	3,562.99	-1.596

* Significant at or beyond .05 level of confidence.
** Significant at or beyond .01 level of confidence.

PCDISP90 = Per capita disposable income (code 050), after taxes   1990
PCDISP91 = Per capita disposable income (code 050), after taxes   1991
PCDISP92 = Per capita disposable income (code 050), after taxes   1992
PCDISP93 = Per capita disposable income (code 050), after taxes   1993
PCDISP94 = Per capita disposable income (code 050), after taxes   1994
PCDISP95 = Per capita disposable income (code 050), after taxes   1995
PCDISP96 = Per capita disposable income (code 050), after taxes   1996
PCDISP97 = Per capita disposable income (code 050), after taxes   1997
PCDISP98 = Per capita disposable income (code 050), after taxes   1998
PCDISP99 = Per capita disposable income (code 050), after taxes   1999
PCDISP00 = Per capita disposable income (code 050), after taxes   2000
PCDISP01 = Per capita disposable income (code 050), after taxes   2001

Addendum and   ***   On the internet   http://www.bea.gov/bea/regional/spi/action.cfm

Appendix I
Health Care and Other Assistance:
Tables 34 - 37

PAYENROL	Significantly more dollars each Medicare enrollee in high murder states	1999
NOCOVER	Significantly higher percent population no health insurance in high murder	1999
CHINOCOV	Significantly higher percent children no health insurance in high murder	1999
AIDSPT	Significantly higher number AIDS cases pr 1,000 population high murder	1998
SYPHILPT	Significantly more syphilis cases per 1,000 population in high murder states	1998
TBPT	Significantly more tuberculosis cases per population in high murder states	1998
MCIGARET	Significantly higher percent males who smoke in high murder states	1998
FCIGARET	Significantly higher percent females who smoke in high murder states	1998
OBESITY	Significantly higher percent persons at risk of obesity in high murder states	1999
TREATFAC	Significantly more drug and alcohol treatment facilities high murder states	1997
PCDRUABU	Significantly higher percent clients in treatment for drugs in high murder	1997
DOCTORS	No difference in physicians per 100,000 population	1998
HOSPBEDP	No difference in hospital beds per 1,000 population	1998
HELP89	No difference in per capita expenditures devoted to cash assistance	1989
HELP90	No difference in per capita expenditures devoted to cash assistance	1990
HELP91	No difference in per capita expenditures devoted to cash assistance	1991
HELP92	No difference in per capita expenditures devoted to cash assistance	1992
HELP93	No difference in per capita expenditures devoted to cash assistance	1993
HELP94	No difference in per capita expenditures devoted to cash assistance	1994
HELP95	No difference in per capita expenditures devoted to cash assistance	1995
HELP96	No difference in per capita expenditures devoted to cash assistance	1996
HELP97	No difference in per capita expenditures devoted to cash assistance	1997
HELP98	No difference in per capita expenditures devoted to cash assistance	1998
HELP99	No difference in per capita expenditures devoted to cash assistance	1999
HELP00	No difference in per capita expenditures devoted to cash assistance	1900
MEDICA90	No difference in per capita expenditures devoted to Medicaid	1990
MEDICA91	No difference in per capita expenditures devoted to Medicaid	1991
MEDICA92	No difference in per capita expenditures devoted to Medicaid	1992
MEDICA93	No difference in per capita expenditures devoted to Medicaid	1993
MEDICA94	No difference in per capita expenditures devoted to Medicaid	1994
MEDICA95	No difference in per capita expenditures devoted to Medicaid	1995
MEDICA96	No difference in per capita expenditures devoted to Medicaid	1996

MEDICA97	No difference in per capita expenditures devoted to Medicaid	1997
MEDICA98	No difference in per capita expenditures devoted to Medicaid	1998
MEDICA99	No difference in per capita expenditures devoted to Medicaid	1999
MEDICAID	No difference per capita expenditures for Medicaid	1989-2000
SUBABUPC	No difference in spending for substance abuse per capita	2000
CASHHELP	No difference average per capita expenditures for cash assistance	1989-2000
MEDICAID	No difference average per capita expenditure for Medicaid	1989-2000

Table 34

Comparison of Mean Values for Health Related Variables
in 25 High Murder Rate States and 25 Low Murder Rate States with the "t" Statistic

Variables Health Care	Table Appendix	25 High Rate States Mean	25 Low Rate States Mean	25 High SD	25 Low SD	"t" value
PAYENROL	G.227	5,213.36	4,264.60	976.96	1,006.76	3.382 **
PAYRECIP	G.230	3,561.68	4,151.33	1,164.78	1,216.02	-1.751
NOCOVER	G.231	17.10	12.94	3.75	3.03	4.310**
CHINOCOV	G.232	16.70	11.35	4.77	3.82	4.374**
DOCTORS	G.233	226.36	242.32	53.79	61.25	-.979
HOSPBEDP	G.256	3.13	3.36	.73	1.24	-.809
AIDSPT	G.236	.15	.08	.10	.07	2.992**
SYPHILPT	G.238	.18	.03	.12	.04	5.930**
TBPT	G.240	.07	.03	.02	.03	4.259**
MCIGARET	G.241	27.55	23.70	2.75	3.80	4.109**
FCIGARET	G.242	22.02	20.16	2.64	2.76	2.435*
OBESITY	G.360	35.00	32.29	3.56	3.38	2.761**

* Significant at or beyond .05 level of confidence.
** Significant at or beyond .01 level of confidence.

PAYENROL	= Dollars each Medicare enrollee		1999
PAYRECIP	= Dollars Medicaid each recipient		1999
NOCOVER	= Percent of population with no health insurance		1998
CHINOCOV	= Percent of children with no health insurance		1998
DOCTORS	= Physicians per 100,000 population		1998
HOSPBEDP	= Hospital beds per 1,000 population		1998
AIDSPT	= Number of AIDS cases per 1,000 population		1998
SYPHILPT	= Number of syphilis cases per 1,000 population		1998
TBPT	= Number of tuberculosis cases per 1,000 population		1998
MCIGARET	= Percent males who smoke		1998
FCIGARET	= Percent females who smoke		1998
OBESITY	= Percent at risk of being overweight		1999

Table 35

Comparison of Mean Values for Cash Assistance
in 25 High Murder Rate States and 25 Low Murder Rate States with the "t" Statistic

Variables Cash	Table Appendix	25 High Rate States Mean	25 Low Rate States Mean	25 High SD	25 Low SD	"t" value
HELP89	G.594	62.25	70.95	51.73	37.06	-.684
HELP90	G.601	75.47	74.97	63.93	37.82	.034
HELP91	G.608	76.64	78.68	62.55	40.67	-.137
HELP92	G.615	91.56	91.45	74.81	50.19	.006
HELP93	G.622	90.40	93.27	72.55	51.68	-.161
HELP94	G.629	91.08	90.05	79.13	46.36	.056
HELP95	G.636	84.32	85.79	78.61	51.78	-.078
HELP96	G.643	73.64	80.58	55.53	46.14	-.480
HELP97	G.650	71.60	77.68	69.28	45.38	-.367
HELP98	G.657	69.58	76.26	73.58	55.74	-.362
HELP99	G.664	62.22	69.86	68.68	45.11	-.465
HELP00	G.671	59.81	72.51	68.47	48.61	-.756

*   Significant at or beyond .05 level of confidence.
**   Significant at or beyond .01 level of confidence.

HELP89	= Per capita expenditures of total funds devoted to cash assistance	1989
HELP90	= Per capita expenditures of total funds devoted to cash assistance	1990
HELP91	= Per capita expenditures of total funds devoted to cash assistance	1991
HELP92	= Per capita expenditures of total funds devoted to cash assistance	1992
HELP93	= Per capita expenditures of total funds devoted to cash assistance	1993
HELP94	= Per capita expenditures of total funds devoted to cash assistance	1994
HELP95	= Per capita expenditures of total funds devoted to cash assistance	1995
HELP96	= Per capita expenditures of total funds devoted to cash assistance	1996
HELP97	= Per capita expenditures of total funds devoted to cash assistance	1997
HELP98	= Per capita expenditures of total funds devoted to cash assistance	1998
HELP99	= Per capita expenditures of total funds devoted to cash assistance	1999
HELP00	= Per capita expenditures of total funds devoted to cash assistance	2000

Table 36

Comparison of Mean Values for Medicaid
in 25 High Murder Rate States and 25 Low Murder Rate States with the "t" Statistic

Variables Medicaid	Table Appendix	25 High Rate States Mean	25 Low Rate States Mean	25 High SD	25 Low SD	"t" value
MEDICA89	G.595	164.51	196.30	75.23	71.99	-1.527
MEDICA90	G.602	226.80	225.61	59.44	72.75	-.063
MEDICA91	G.609	279.19	270.60	67.70	81.91	-.404
MEDICA92	G.616	365.14	377.65	91.91	153.65	-.349
MEDICA93	G.623	434.02	428.73	116.54	169.92	-.128
MEDICA94	G.630	481.38	457.06	162.26	151.35	-.548
MEDICA95	G.637	482.62	473.68	172.69	141.37	-.200
MEDICA96	G.644	563.59	518.62	226.95	152.50	-.822
MEDICA97	G.651	542.90	525.39	165.84	183.33	-.354
MEDICA98	G.658	565.26	553.78	181.53	176.02	-.227
MEDICA99	G.665	582.68	602.04	184.72	173.95	-.381
MEDICA00	G.672	612.32	653.65	195.39	231.29	-.683

*   Significant at or beyond .05 level of confidence.
**   Significant at or beyond .01 level of confidence.

MEDICA89	= Per capita expenditures of total funds devoted to Medicaid	1989
MEDICA90	= Per capita expenditures of total funds devoted to Medicaid	1990
MEDICA91	= Per capita expenditures of total funds devoted to Medicaid	1991
MEDICA92	= Per capita expenditures of total funds devoted to Medicaid	1992
MEDICA93	= Per capita expenditures of total funds devoted to Medicaid	1993
MEDICA94	= Per capita expenditures of total funds devoted to Medicaid	1994
MEDICA95	= Per capita expenditures of total funds devoted to Medicaid	1995
MEDICA96	= Per capita expenditures of total funds devoted to Medicaid	1996
MEDICA97	= Per capita expenditures of total funds devoted to Medicaid	1997
MEDICA98	= Per capita expenditures of total funds devoted to Medicaid	1998
MEDICA99	= Per capita expenditures of total funds devoted to Medicaid	1999
MEDICA00	= Per capita expenditures of total funds devoted to Medicaid	2000

Table 37

Comparison of Mean Values for Abuse Clinic Variables
in 25 High Murder Rate States and 25 Low Murder Rate States with the "t" Statistic

Variables Abuse	Table Appendix	25 High Rate States Mean	25 Low Rate States Mean	25 High SD	25 Low SD	"t" value
TREATFAC	G.417	292.20	138.00	315.77	112.93	2.299*
PCLIENTS	G.419	.30	.36	.14	.16	-1.451
PCALCABU	G.420	28.96	33.15	7.90	11.28	-1.798
PCDRUABU	G.421	30.93	21.95	9.77	9.84	3.239**
PCDRUALC	G.422	40.49	44.90	8.02	9.15	-1.810
PCPAROLE	G.424	.19	.14	.14	.16	1.133
SUBABUPC	G.254	262.86	272.52	89.34	88.65	-.364
CASHHELP	G.678	75.72	80.17	64.56	42.94	-.287
MEDICAID	G.679	441.70	440.26	126.44	128.20	.040

*   Significant at or beyond .05 level of confidence.
**   Significant at or beyond .01 level of confidence.

TREATFAC	= Number drug and alcohol treatment facilities	1997
PCLIENTS	= Percent state population in treatment for drug or alcohol abuse	1997
PCALCABU	= Percent of clients in treatment for alcohol abuse	1997
PCDRUABU	= Percent of clients in treatment for drug abuse	1997
PCDRUALC	= Percent of clients in treatment for drug and alcohol abuse	1997
PCPAROLE	= Percent of state population on parole	1999
SUBABUPC	= Spending for substance abuse, per capita	2000
CASHHELP	= Average per capita expenditure for cash assistance	1989-2000
MEDICAID	= Average per capita expenditure for Medicaid	1989-2000

Appendix J
Highways and Transportation:
Tables 38 - 39

HIWAYFND	Significantly higher state highway funds high murder rate states	1998
HIWAYTRS	Significantly higher federal grants (HTF) per capita in low murder states	1998
GASTAX	Significantly higher state gasoline tax in low murder rate states	1998
HIWAY96	Significantly higher per capita expenditures for transportation low murder	1996
BRIDGDEF	No difference in percent of bridges deficient	1998
HIWAYFED	No difference in federal grants (FTA) per capita	1998
HIWAY91	No difference in per capita expenditures total funds devoted transportation	1991
HIWAY95	No difference in per capita expenditures total funds devoted transportation	1995
HIWAY99	No difference in per capita expenditures total funds devoted transportation	1999
HIWAY00	No difference in per capita expenditures total funds devoted transportation	2000

Table 38

Comparison of Mean Values for Highway Related Variables
in 25 High Murder Rate States and 25 Low Murder Rate States with the "t" Statistic

Variables Highway	Table Appendix	25 High Rate States Mean	25 Low Rate States Mean	25 High SD	25 Low SD	"t" value
BRIDGDEF	G.182	14.76	14.81	9.23	5.49	-.024
BRIDGOBS	G.183	13.75	15.75	4.29	8.58	-1.045
HIWAYFND	G.184	2,122.40	1,087.92	1,661.70	956.68	2.698**
HIWAYFED	G.185	10.04	12.40	8.70	13.37	-.737
HIWAYTRS	G.186	85.46	120.58	66.09	56.73	-2.016*
GASTAX	G.187	18.02	22.35	4.09	6.08	-2.953**
ALLOTHER	G.682	871.23	1,040.55	453.10	412.18	-1.382

* Significant at or beyond .05 level of confidence.
** Significant at or beyond .01 level of confidence.

BRIDGDEF	= Percent of bridges deficient	1998
BRIDGOBS	= Percent of bridges obsolete	1998
HIWAYFND	= State highway funds	1998
HIWAYFED	= Federal grants (FTA) per capita	1998
HIWAYTRS	= Federal grants (HTF) per capita	1998
GASTAX	= State gasoline tax (cents per gallon)	1998
ALLOTHER	= Average per capita expenditure for all other items	1989-2000

Table 39

Comparison of Mean Values for Highways and Transportation
in 25 High Murder Rate States and 25 Low Murder Rate States with the "t" Statistic

Variables Highways	Table Appendix	25 High Rate States Mean	25 Low Rate States Mean	25 High SD	25 Low SD	"t" value
HIWAY89	G.597	199.32	249.85	140.66	93.58	-1.495
HIWAY90	G.604	231.73	292.12	182.31	156.56	-1.257
HIWAY91	G.611	253.53	300.93	214.05	172.08	-.863
HIWAY92	G.618	255.32	319.11	220.74	178.31	-1.124
HIWAY93	G.625	256.58	310.64	196.25	158.16	-1.072
HIWAY94	G.632	268.04	322.17	235.87	128.69	-1.007
HIWAY95	G.639	272.64	323.35	238.98	123.85	-.942
HIWAY96	G.646	264.08	338.86	108.22	116.67	-2.350*
HIWAY97	G.653	284.49	348.40	188.96	140.75	-1.356
HIWAY98	G.660	305.31	357.54	170.86	133.30	-1.205
HIWAY99	G.667	332.34	378.34	308.16	128.29	-.689
HIWAY00	G.674	350.22	381.90	351.21	109.53	-.431
HIGHWAYS	G.681	272.80	326.93	209.16	124.72	-1.111

*   Significant at or beyond .05 level of confidence.
**   Significant at or beyond .01 level of confidence.

HIWAY89	= Per capita expenditures of total funds devoted to transportation	1989
HIWAY90	= Per capita expenditures of total funds devoted to transportation	1990
HIWAY91	= Per capita expenditures of total funds devoted to transportation	1991
HIWAY92	= Per capita expenditures of total funds devoted to transportation	1992
HIWAY93	= Per capita expenditures of total funds devoted to transportation	1993
HIWAY94	= Per capita expenditures of total funds devoted to transportation	1994
HIWAY95	= Per capita expenditures of total funds devoted to transportation	1995
HIWAY96	= Per capita expenditures of total funds devoted to transportation	1996
HIWAY97	= Per capita expenditures of total funds devoted to transportation	1997
HIWAY98	= Per capita expenditures of total funds devoted to transportation	1998
HIWAY99	= Per capita expenditures of total funds devoted to transportation	1999
HIWAY00	= Per capita expenditures of total funds devoted to transportation	2000
HIGHWAYS	= Average per capita expenditure for transportation	1989-2000

Appendix K
General Factors:
Table 40

GOVERNMT   Significantly more problems with procurement of funds high murder rate states

EXPEND   Significantly more problems with expenditures of funds high murder rate states

CRIME   Significantly more problems with crime rate high murder rate states

PUNISH   Significantly more problems with punishment high murder rate states

HIWAYDEA   Significantly more problems with highway fatalities high murder rate states

TRAUMA   Significantly more problems with traumatic deaths high murder rate states

HEALTH   Significantly more problems with health factors high murder rate states

MEDICAL   Significantly more problems with health care costs high murder rate states

TEENPROB   Significantly more teenage problems in high murder rate states

EDUCACHI   Significantly more problems educational achievement high murder rate states

EDUCSUPP   Significantly more problems educational support in high murder rate states

WORK   Significantly more problems work and employment high murder rate states

ECONOMIC   Significantly more problems with economic opportunities high murder rate

SUMMARY   Significantly more problems with summation of all factors high murder rate

Table 40

Comparison of Mean Values for Problems Associated With General Factors
in 25 High Murder Rate States and 25 Low Murder Rate States with the "t" Statistic

Variables Gen Factors	Table Appendix	25 High Rate States Mean	25 Low Rate States Mean	25 High SD	25 Low SD	"t" value
GOVERNMT	G.687	29.63	23.18	6.27	9.13	2.656**
EXPEND	G.688	28.81	23.64	6.64	6.55	2.665**
CRIME	G.689	30.22	22.84	9.08	11.55	2.332*
PROTECT	G.690	27.66	24.29	7.55	7.97	1.462
PUNISH	G.691	32.80	21.40	7.06	7.32	5.353**
DEATH	G.692	28.80	23.65	12.27	11.20	1.508
HIWAYDEA	G.693	29.98	22.98	4.07	4.15	5.770**
TRAUMA	G.694	34.88	20.23	7.43	13.22	5.015**
HEALTH	G.695	31.38	22.19	7.96	7.67	4.009**
MEDICAL	G.696	30.71	22.57	6.53	6.63	4.190**
TEENPROB	G.697	32.96	21.30	7.47	7.20	5.427**
EDUCACHI	G.698	34.32	20.54	8.78	8.08	5.613**
EDUCSUPP	G.699	32.90	21.34	7.18	6.79	5.659**
WORK	G.700	28.65	23.73	5.29	4.81	3.353**
ECONOMIC	G.701	31.25	22.27	6.84	7.26	3.594**
SUMMARY	G.702	464.93	336.13	62.17	50.13	7.992**

*   Significant at or beyond .05 level of confidence.
**   Significant at or beyond .01 level of confidence.

GOVERNMT = General factor (8 variables) problems with government procurement of funds
EXPEND = General factor (7 variables) problems with government expenditures of funds
CRIME = General factor (8 variables) problems with crime rates
PROTECT = General factor (5 variables) problems with police protection
PUNISH = General factor (11 variables) problems with punishment for crimes
DEATH = General factor (6 variables) problems with death from natural causes
HIWAYDEA = General factor (11 variables) problems with highway fatalities
TRAUMA = General factor (2 variables) problems with traumatic deaths
HEALTH = General factor (8 variables) problems with health factors
MEDICAL = General factor (8 variables) problems with health care costs
TEENPROB = General factor (9 variables) problems of teenagers
EDUCACHI = General factor (4 variables) problems with educational achievement
EDUCSUPP = General factor (9 variables) problems with support for education
WORK = General factor (17 variables) problems with work and employment
ECONOMIC = General factor (7 variables) problems with economic opportunities
SUMMARY = General factor (15 factors) summation of all problems with factor scores

References

Chapter 1

1. Eric Hoffer, *The True Believers* (New York, Harper Collins, 1951).

2. John Hersey, "The Triumph of Numbers," *The Atlantic Monthly*, vol. 246, October 1980, pp. 78-84.

3. Jack Frymier and Arliss Roaden, *Cultures of the States: A Handbook on Effectiveness of State Governments*, (Lanham, MD. and Oxford: Scarecrow Press, Inc., 2003), 411 pp.

4. Frymier and Roaden, Cultures, p. 228 and p. 253.

Chapter 2

1. Jack Frymier and Arliss Roaden, *Cultures of the States: A Handbook on Effectiveness of State Governments*, (Lanham, MD. and Oxford: Scarecrow Press, Inc., 2003), 411 pp.

Chapter 3

1. Jack Frymier and Arliss Roaden, *Cultures of the States: A Handbook on Effectiveness of State Governments*, (Lanham, MD. and Oxford: Scarecrow Press, Inc., 2003), p. 227 and various versions of *Statistical Abstract of the United States* covering many years.

2. *Historical Statistics of the United States: Colonial times to 1970, Part 2* (Washington, D.C.: U..S. Department of Commerce, Bureau of the Census, 1975), p. 1140.

3. Ibid., p. 719.

Chapter 4

1. James Alan Fox, "Trends in Juvenile Violence: A Report to the United States Attorney General on Current and Future Rates of Juvenile Offending," p 4. Prepared for the Bureau of Justice Statistics, United States Department of Justice, Washington, D.C., March 1996, 17 pp.

From the internet: URL - http://www.ojp.usdoj.gov/bjs/pub/pdf/tjvfox2.pdf

2. Jack Frymier and Arliss Roaden, *Cultures of the States: A Handbook on Effectiveness of State Governments* (Lanham, MD. and Oxford: Scarecrow Press, Inc., 2003), p. 120.

3. Margaret A. Zahn and Katherine M. Jamieson, "Changing Patterns of Homicide and Social Policy," *Homicide Studies*, vol. 1, No. 2, May 1997, pp. 190-196.

4. Alfred Blumstein and Richard Rosenfeld, "Explaining Recent trends in U.S. Homicide Rates, *The Journal of Criminal Law and Criminology*, vol. 88, No. 4, 1998, pp. 1175-1216.

5. Lauren B. Alloy and Martin E. P. Seligman, "On the Cognitive Component of Learned Helplessness and Depression," in Gordon H. Bower (ed.), *The Psychology of Learning and Motivation* (New York: Academic Press, 1979), p. 120. Emphasis added.

6. Mark Twain, "From Bombay to Missouri," *Following the Equator* (Hartford: The AmericanPublishing Co., 1897).

7. Harriet Beecher Stowe, "A Reply to the Address of the Women of England," *The Atlantic Monthly*, (January 1863), pp, 120-134.

8. Henry Steele Commager (ed.), "The Earliest Protest Against Slavery: 1688," *Documents of American History,* vol. 1, Fifth Edition, (New York: Appleton-Century-Crofts, Inc.,1949), p. 37.

9. Commager, "The Association: 1774," *Documents,* p. 85.

10. Commager, "The Quock Walker Case: 1783," *Documents,* p. 110.

11. Commager, "The Northwest Ordinance: 1786," *Documents,* p. 132.

12. Commager, "The Constitution of the United States," *Documents,* pp. 138-149

13. *Chisholm v. Georgia*, 2 Dall. (2. U.S.) 419 (1793).

14. Johnny H. Killian, (ed.), *The Constitution of the United States of America* (Washington, D.C., U.S. Government Printing Office, 1987), p. 1427.

15. Commager, "Act to Prohibit the Importation of Slaves: 1807," *Documents,* p. 197.

16. Commager, "The Kentucky and Virginia Resolutions: 1798" *Documents,* pp. 178-183.

17. Commager, "The Missouri Compromise: 1819-1821," *Documents,* pp. 224-227.

18. Commager, "Marbury v. Madison: 1803," *Documents,* pp. 191-195.

19. Don E. Fehrenbacher, *The Dred Scott Case* (Oxford and New York: Oxford University Press, 1978), Chapters 13 and 14.

20. Commager, "Jackson's Proclamation to the People of South Carolina: 1832," *Documents,* pp. 262-268.

21. Commager, "South Carolina's Reply to Jackson's Proclamation: 1832," *Documents,* pp. 191-195.

22. Commager, "South Carolina Resolutions on Abolitionist Propaganda: 1835," *Documents,* pp. 281-282.

23. Commager, "The Compromise of 1850," *Documents,* pp. 319-323.

24. Commager, "Trial of Mrs. Douglas for Teaching Colored Children to Read: 1853," *Documents,* pp. 327-329.

25. Commager, "Lincoln's House Divided Speech: 1858," *Documents,* pp. 345-347

26. Commager, "Ableman v. Booth: 1859," *Documents,* pp. 358-361.

27. Commager, "John Brown's Last Speech: 1859," *Documents,* pp. 361-362.

28. Commager, "Resolutions on Secession from Floyd County, Georgia: 1860," *Documents,* pp. 362-363.

29. Commager, "Mississippi Resolutions on Secession: 1860," *Documents,* pp. 371-372.

30. Commager, "The Constitution of the Confederate States of America: 1861," *Documents,* pp. 376-384.

31. Commager, "Emancipation Proclamation: 1863," *Documents,* pp. 420-421.

32. Commager, "Lincoln's Proclamation on the Wade-Davis Bill: 1864," *Documents,* p. 239.

33. Eric Foner, *Reconstruction: America's Unfinished Revolution, 1863-1877* (New York: Harper and Row, Publishers, 1988), p. 70.

34. Commager, "Lincoln's Terms of Peace: March 27, 1865," *Documents,* pp. 443-444.

35. Jean Edward Smith, *Grant* (New York: A Touchstone Book by Simon & Schuster, 2001), p. 393.

36. Douglas Southall Freeman, *Lee*, as abridged in one volume by Richard Harwell (New York: Collier Books, 1991), p. 493.

37. James P. Boyd, *The Life of General William T. Sherman* (Publisher's Union, 1891), p. 439.

38. Smith, *Grant*, pp. 407-408.

39. Smith, *Grant*, p. 410.

40. Killian, *The Constitution*, p. 1453.

41. Killian, *The Constitution*, p. 1455.

42. Killian, *The Constitution*, p. 1456.

43. Smith, *Grant*, p. 416.

44. Smith, *Grant*, p. 418.

45. Henry Steele Commager, (ed.), "The Freedmen's Bureau: 1865," *Documents of American History,* vol. 2, Fifth Edition, (New York: Appleton-Century-Crofts, Inc., 1949), p. 1.

46. Commager, "Black Code of Mississippi: 1865," *Documents*, pp. 2-5.

47. Commager, "The Civil Rights Act: 1866," *Documents*, pp. 14-15.

48. Commager, "Veto of the Civil Rights Act: 1866," *Documents*, pp. 15-18.

49. Killian, *The Constitution*, p. 1467.

50. Smith, *Grant*, p. 423.

51. Smith, *Grant*, p. 543.

52. Smith, *Grant*, p. 544.

53. Smith, *Grant*, p. 545.

54. Killian, *The Constitution*, p. 1823.

55. Smith, *Grant*, p. 546.

56. Smith, *Grant*, p. 562.

57. Smith, *Grant*, pp. 562-563.

58. Killian, *The Constitution*, p. 1467.

59. Killian, *The Constitution*, pp. 1467-1468.

60. Killian, *The Constitution*, pp. 1470.

61. Killian, *The Constitution*, pp. 1461-1731.

62. Killian, *The Constitution*, pp. 1695.

63. Killian, *The Constitution*, pp. 1732-1733.

64. Rocco J. Tresolini, *Justice and the Supreme Court* (Philadelphia: J. B. Lippincott Company, 1963), pp. 52-53.

65. Stanley Milgram, on the Internet:
http://www.barnabesministry.com/church-milgram_obedience.html

66. Stanley Milgram, *Obedience to Authority* (New York: Harper & Row, Publishers, 1974), 234 pp.

67. Daniel J. Goldhagen, *Hitler's Willing Executioners* (New York, Alfred A. Knopf, 1996), 622 pp.

Chapter 5

1. Michael R. Gardner, *Harry Truman and Civil Rights* (Carbondale and Edwardsville, IL: Southern Illinois University Press, 2002), pp. 16.

2. Ibid., p. 18.

3. Ibid., Chapters 2 through 7.

4. Johnny H. Killian, (ed.), ***The Constitution of the United States of America*** (Washington, D.C., U.S. Government Printing Office, 1987), p. 1734.

5. Ibid., p. 1735.

6. Ibid., pp. 1735-1736.

7. Ibid., 1736-1737.

8. Gardner, ***Harry Truman***, p. 82 and p. 127.

9. Doris Goodwin Kearns, ***Lyndon Johnson and the American Dream*** (New York: St. Martins Griffin, 1976 and 1991), 435 pp.

10. George F. Kennan, ***Memoirs: 1925-1950***, (New York: Pantheon Books, 1967), Chapter 11, "The Long Telegram," Chapter 15, "The X-Article," and Annex C, "***Excerpts from*** Telegraphic Message from Moscow of February 22, 1946."

11. Ibid., Chapter 14, "The Marshall Plan."

12. Ibid., Chapter 13, "The Truman Doctrine."

13. Gardner, ***Harry Truman***, p. 105.

14. Ibid., p. 95. See also "Truman Doctrine," The Avalon Project at Yale Law School, on the internet: http://www.yale.edu/lawweb/Avalon/trudoc.htm

15. Killian, ***The Constitution***, p. 1734.

16. Gardner, ***Harry Truman***, p. 138 ff.

17. Lauren B. Alloy and Martin E. P. Seligman, "On the Cognitive Component of Learned Helplessness and Depression," in Gordon H. Bower (ed.), ***The Psychology of Learning and Motivation*** (New York: Academic Press, 1979), p. 120. Emphasis added.

18. Neal E. Miller. "The Frustration-Aggression Hypothesis," on the internet at http://psychclassics.yorku.ca/Frust/Agg/miller.htm. See also ***Psychological Review***, vol. 48, pp. 337-342.

19. Ibid.

20. Robyn Marks, "My Turn: Raising a Son—With Men on the Fringes," ***Newsweek*** (July

19, 2004), p. 12.

21. Jack Frymier, "Developing a Sense of Responsibility," *Growing Up Is Risky Business,* (Bloomington, IN: Phi Delta Kappa, 1992), pp. 71-78.

22. . Pamela M. Wharton and Jacqueline J. Goodnow, "The Nature of Responsibility: Children Understanding 'Your Job,'" *Child Development*, vol. 62 (1991), pp. 156-165.

23. Tjert Olthof, Tamara J. Ferguson, and Annemieke Luiten, "Personal Responsibility: Antecedents of Anger and Blame Reactions in Children," *Child Development*, vol. 60 (1989), pp. 1328-1336.

24. Larry Bartlett, "Legal Responsibilities of Students: Study Shows School Officials Also Win Court Decisions," *NASSP Bulletin*, vol. 69, no. 479 (March 1985), pp. 39-47.

25. Shirley Kane Lewis and Elizabeth Lawrence-Patterson, "Locus of Control of Children with Learning Disabilities and Perceived Locus of Control by Significant Others," *Journal of Learning Disabilities*, vol. 22, no. 4 (April 1989), pp. 255-257.

26. Elizabeth Ramsey, et al., "Parent Management Practices and School Adjustment," *School Psychology Review*, vol. 18, no. 4 (1989), pp. 513-525.

27. Gunter Krampen, "Perceived Childrearing Practices and the Development of Locus of Control in Early Adolescence," *International Journal of Behavioral Development*, vol. 12, no. 2 (1989), pp. 177-193.

28. C. William Garner and Ernest G. Cole, "The Achievement of Students in Low-SES Settings: An Investigation of the Relationship Between Locus of Control and Field Dependence," *Urban Education*, vol. 21, no. 2 (1986), pp. 189-206.

29. V. Lee Hamilton, Phyllis C. Blumfield, Hiroshi Akoh, and Kanae Miura, "Japanese and American Children's Reasons for Things They Do in School," *American Educational Research Journal*, vol. 26, no. 4 (Winter 1989), pp. 545-571.

30. Stephen J. Lepere, et al., "Children's Perceptions of Social Ability: Social Cognition and Behavioral Outcomes in the Face of Social Rejection, *Child Study Journal*, vol. 19, no. 4 (1989), pp. 259-271.

About the Authors

Jack Frymier received his Bachelor's and Master's degrees from the University of Miami, and his Doctorate from the University of Florida. He served in the U.S. Army during World War II and the Korean War. He has been a public school teacher, administrator, university professor, and researcher, and is currently Professor Emeritus at Ohio State University.

Arliss Roaden is Executive Director Emeritus of the Tennessee Higher Education Commission, President Emeritus of Tennessee Technological University, and former Dean of the Graduate School at Ohio State University.

www.ingramcontent.com/pod-product-compliance
Lightning Source LLC
Chambersburg PA
CBHW080413290526
45791CB00008BA/2255